Body, Mime, and Soul

WHEN ACTIONS SPEAK
LOUDER THAN WORDS

To Victoria:
Never stop dancing
on the skinny branches!

10-30-2020

Ken Alcorn

ISBN 978-1-64300-987-2 (Paperback)
ISBN 978-1-64300-988-9 (Digital)

Covenant Books, Inc.
11661 Hwy 707
Murrells Inlet, SC 29576
www.covenantbooks.com

This book is dedicated to
my mother, Jane W. Alcorn; my late father, George M. Alcorn;
my wife, Beth; and my children, James, Jeremy, Joshua, and Jenna.

CONTENTS

Far better it is to dare mighty things, to win glorious triumph, even though checkered by failure, than to take rank with those poor spirits who neither enjoy much nor suffer much, because they live in the gray twilight that knows not victory or defeat.

—Theodore Roosevelt

INTRODUCTION

For nearly ten full years, during the 1980s, I traveled from town to town, touring city to city, university to clubs, festivals to schools, and conferences to conventions, performing my one-man mime show. Somewhere in the middle of my high school career was planted the seed of being an actor, though at that time, being a musician seemed to guide the trajectory of my future. Sitting in a practice room gave way to the draw of the stage, a pursuit that would lead to years of training.

What had been anticipated as being a parallel track in the climb to the top of my acting career turned out to be a different road entirely leading to points unforeseen, and in truth, why should they have been expected? At any one of those points, it might have been supposed prudent to go back to New York in pursuit of a career on Broadway. That didn't happen. Being master of my ship on this course into the future created a great satisfaction. Sure, there were times of self-doubt, and maybe it appeared that avoiding the challenge of being a New York actor manifested out of fear by continued travel and pursuing a different direction. Might this, again, be my own self-doubt masking the fear of insufficient knowledge and talent to be considered a true artist, fearful to be exposed as a fraud and pretender?

No, it wasn't fear or avoidance, though those demon thoughts had to be mollified. Finding a way to distinguish myself in a different light than any other performing artist determined my climb. Then one thing led to another and continued as life does. After the millions of little choices along the way with some really big ones thrown in, because of shifting priorities, suddenly, it almost seemed, after years on the road as a traveling entertainer, the road stopped on the doorstep with the door opening to a new role of a stay-at-home father.

Being an actor, let alone a mime, carries with it an undertone of denigration, until success changes the perception and then the condescension switches to praise. And the same holds true for a stay-at-home dad. The undercurrent of our culture reduces the man taking on the role of the househusband as a stigmatized ne'er-do-well. Many men think this is not a manly vocation for a real man, and those who do follow this path are perceived as weak.

As a deacon in my church, I answered many questions from men wondering if doing the traditional woman's role of child-rearing was, indeed, taking on the role of head of the household, as my wife, being a surgeon, took on the role of the primary income provider. This seemed to fly in the face of traditional thought.

Had this been a younger man, with no history of a career and seven years of college, there is no telling the disdain to be endured. For over ten years, millions had seen me work, maybe not hitting the big time or securing a future with a few large paydays, but to survive as an artist on the road for that length of time justified my belief that success had been achieved. Having acquired a sense of surety about myself in those years fortified the feeling of self-worth enough to not be affected by the naysayers about a man staying home with his children.

To my belief, a man does not abdicate his leadership role by choosing to raise his children. He is no less a man because his wife does something that produces a paycheck larger than what is available to him at that time, stay at home or otherwise. It does not mean circumstances won't change in the future. On the contrary, it takes a man quite sure of himself to go against the grain of public perception. It takes a strong man to put his ego aside because the job division of his family isn't as important as his commitment to his family.

My father passed away a couple of years ago. I miss his stories and wish details could be recalled that are now gone with him. My children know a few of my stories, but there are so many that they do not know. What started as a desire to have a written documentation chronicling some of my experiences in hopes that a piece of me travels into the future for my children and theirs expanded to include stories beyond my touring years. Without the encouragement along the way from those who knew me before my mime years and the years since, the possibility that my story would be passed down by word of mouth would lose even more details than are already lost, just as many of my father's stories have been. Being a mime, word of mouth could not be trusted. My life has not been bound by traditional choices.

So this simple idea has evolved from how I chose to become a mime, because there are few books to chronicle something like that, to include my life as a stay-at-home father, also with few books dealing with this subject either.

Entertaining my audience during the performance of my mime show and giving them food for thought were of equal importance to me. And so it is with this book. I definitely want you to be entertained by the foibles and stories that I tell. But I also want you to understand the heartaches, the setbacks, and the obstacles that molded me and from where I found strength, faith, and courage along the way. And in the telling, if you were to walk away with enhanced perceptions you may not have considered, that is all the better.

My path has had many twists and turns with ups and downs and steps forward and steps backward. After all, not many people aspire to be a mime. It did not start that way.

Likewise, leaving the stage to become a stay-at-home father did not formulate out of some preconceived master plan for my life. Not many men grow up thinking that twenty-five to thirty years of his life will be dedicated to taking on the traditional role of a stay-at-home mother. No, it did not start that way either.

I invite you to read the words of a man who did not speak, only to find his voice in the middle of an empty space, on the pages of a notebook, within the harmonies of a piano, and in the paint on a canvas, only to give up that particular voice, temporarily, to guide his children in finding theirs. It is my hope that you enjoy my recounting the highlights and lowlights of a journey—how it started, where it led, and one that is yet to see its end.

CHAPTER

1

How Does One End Up a Mime?

So you think I'm just a mime and I'm not supposed to talk
But if you watch me closely I'll show you how to walk
Now I wouldn't want to tell you exactly what to do
But if you watch me closely I'll make a wall for you

I've learned these tricks in college and that's no joke
Lots of people pay me to climb this rope
You may know already that mime has lots of grace
As I create for you by just using space

With only body movements, imagination too
I communicate my concepts and view of life for you
I am an entertainer and if you did not know
I'll need your full attention in the process of my show

The world of mime is waiting so without too much delay
We'll all go on a journey and you'll see what I won't say
My name is Kenny Alcorn, though you may call me Ken
You'll have to watch me closely 'cause I won't speak again

So make yourselves real cozy; you're in for quite a time
I welcome you to my world, that gentle art of mime

The sun had gone down. The pre-show cacophony from the fifty thousand festivalgoers who gathered on the bank of the Tennessee River had just quieted when the massive arch of stage lights dimmed to black allowing me to take my place center stage. There I stood motionless in the center of the darkness on the converted barge to a performance stage moored on the edge of the river. It could very easily swallow up a performer, and I knew it. Dress rehearsal taught that thinking myself twice as large would help fill the stage and be easier to be seen by the audience.

Time slowed for those few moments as I waited with my back to the audience. I shot imaginary energy bolts from my shoulder blades to jolt everyone between me and the back row, easily a couple of hundred yards away.

"Ladies and gentlemen," the announcer's voice reverberated through the sound system, "let's give a Chattanooga Riverbend Festival welcome to Ken Alcorn's *Body, Mime, and Soul*."

The audience erupted into applause. They returned to near silence when "Fantasy" by Earth, Wind and Fire blasted out over the speakers. The lights slowly illuminated the stage to reveal me standing motionless wearing black tights and red leotards and a black hood over my head. A brown leather suitcase with bumper stickers and backstage passes of prior shows plastered randomly over it sat off to the side about ten feet away. Oh, I knew this was different than my hundreds of performances done before. Typically, excitement rather than nervousness built in the moments before I went onstage, and this night was no different in that respect, but my adrenaline was really flowing. Breathing took a noticeable amount of energy to keep steady and calm, just like what my legs demanded in holding an opening pose that contained an imperceptible tremble to anyone but me. I still wouldn't call it nerves, but oh yeah, I was excited. This stage now belonged to me, and I relished in its warmth and glow. My concentration, acute and in the moment, moved from the thought of any audience watching to performing the opening piece as I turned to face them.

After the music stopped and the swell of the applause rose in opposition to the lights fading to black, I held my finishing position. There is a glow that takes a few seconds to fully reach full blackout when the lights go down, so it was important to hold still those few extra moments; otherwise, the effect of the ending would lose its crispness. In the dark, I took my place for my next piece called *Masks*. Now on my knees, forehead touching the stage, and arms to my side, the jazz masterpiece "Take Five" by Dave Brubeck began to play to add a sense of curiousness as the lights came back up.

As if being manipulated by an invisible puppeteer, one arm flung up and then another, and the marionette figure began to move by the pull of the strings. Noticing the relationship of movement to the strings, the marionette appeared to think for himself, discovered his limited ability to move on his own, and yanked the strings off. Finding his balance, he became extremely pleased and discovered his body by feeling its parts, arms, legs, hands, and torso. Then he wrapped his arms around his body and then his head and excitedly placed his hands on his cheeks in an "Oh my" type of pose. It was then that he realized, by feeling around the hooded face, that there was no actual face. Panic set in. What to do? He began to look high and low and all around when the spotlight hit the upright suitcase.

He approached it, inspected it, placed it down on its back and gently, slowly opened it. What's inside? He looked down in the case, back up and out toward the audience, then back down, then up, then down, up, down, up, and down. Reaching in with a dramatic arm swing, this faceless being buried his head into the suitcase and popped up with a mask placed on top of his head, and his body now became a creature that stalked the stage with a nimbleness of a cat. He stopped and, with front and back paws on the ground in a tiger-like stance, surveyed the multitudes with a menacing stare. Suddenly he stood on his hind legs to transform into an apelike animal with the mask still situated on the top of his head, and neck bent forward, the illusion was made of a wild and untamed imp with arms flailing away until he calmed down returning back to bury his head into the suitcase.

The masks were switched, and now the former marionette emerged as a disfigured man who transformed into a boxer getting beat up by his opponent. And so it went on with mask after mask, transformation after transformation, taking on new characteristics to magnify the different emotions and foibles that each new face might indicate, from haughty waiter to gruff politician, to a feeble old man, and to a carefree and innocent child picking a flower. This character enjoyed the flowers' fragrance, then picked its petals throwing them up, and watched them gently float down. When this childlike fellow threw the plucked flower up, to his great chagrin, it plummeted to the ground. He contemplated the physics of it all and then gleefully stomped on the discarded bloom.

Each distinct mask with multiple personalities proved too frustrating, and finally, the disheartened, emancipated marionette became discontent with each false face and lamented not having his own identity. When he ripped off the last mask and in so doing pulled off the black hood, he exposed his natural face in the form of a white-faced mime while concurrently being reattached to the puppeteer's strings, thus leaving him to sway in limbo. As the lights faded to black, the white-faced mime Ken Alcorn had at last been revealed to his audience for the first time.

The sound of appreciation that arose from the sea of people, heretofore quietly attentive, gave me the feeling of a conquering hero fresh from battle. For the next twenty or so minutes, this gratification within took me to an inner place I wished would and could last forever.

The next piece was an interpretation of a life cycle, which led to a skit called *The Burglar*, followed by one named *Romance*, performed standing motionless except the choreography of only white-gloved hands. The performance wrapped up with a vignette entitled *The Dream*. Standing center stage and soaking in the applause isn't a thing I ever became very comfortable with. Maybe the years of training where the importance wasn't the reaction I received but the gratification of performing a thing to my best ability had something to do with that. Yet, here I stood, lingering a few extra seconds than I typically would, enjoying and almost trying to mentally record the moment. On only rare occasions did I ever prolong a bow to absorb more of the applause. Something in me always felt a little unworthy of the praise. Accepting the audience's gratitude is necessary. It allows them to thank the performer or performers. This I have always known and is genuinely the polite thing to do. It is a gift, so to speak. As much as the artist's thankfulness for the opportunity to perform, it is just as important for the audience. It completes the program.

Performing and getting paid for it on top of that seemed plenty for me. Do not misunderstand me. Those few moments at the end of the show were important. The curtain call was not what drove me, though underneath it all the affirmation gave a sense of worthiness. Fifty thousand people cheering for me though transformed even the most reluctant recipient I do believe. We all dream of moments like it, no doubt. Then the glow fades. The return to a normal heartbeat, a business as usual, resumes. There was still the getting out of costume and putting away of my masks and props for the next time to do. The ritual did not change. Except for a sprinkling of backstage congratulations, this mime again retreated silently to his dressing room, this time to the tethered houseboat alongside the converted barge. Crystal Gayle now occupied the spotlight. All eyes were on her now. The mime just smiled and said nothing.

I am a mime. And some may say pantomime. Very few can profess to that. How I developed into one is only part of my story. My story didn't start there and didn't end there. Shifting from an over-the-road mime to a full time father and husband and how that transmutation transpired has created my desire to share my unusual journey. Like an onion, layers will be peeled away exposing my trek a little at a time, only this time using words.

On a few occasions, that *rap* verse spoken over a pulsing drumbeat opened my solo mime show, *Body, Mime, and Soul.* Because it described me and what I did, treated as a prologue then and now, it acted and acts as an introduction. The genre had not been as innovative and mainstream as it is today, when this was written. Some may pass this off as a bad attempt, but I still like it. Why? Because I wrote it! To me, that part alone made it good. And as mentioned, its performance shelf life expired rather quickly. As part of the creative process, playing and molding ideas to something workable took experimentation that led to use or putting them aside maybe to revisit them later or not.

Beginning a mime show with a *rap* song worked in theory only. Trying it a few times by testing it on the audience, the realization that it dampened the impact of my show by breaking an accepted tradition of nonverbal communication that did not create the mystique intended for provided the information needed to ditch this approach for good. Having this printed on a program would have been much more appropriate because it did not interrupt the atmosphere that needed to be established.

If I shoot at the sun I may hit a star. (P. T. Barnum)

The Bait and Switch

The accordion tricked me, or should I say my parents tricked me. As early as five years old, I wanted to play the accordion. Mom and Dad said that through learning the piano first, learning to play the accordion later would be easier. It is now much later, and playing the accordion lost its allure. But as the accordion dream of this five-year-old changed along the way, the piano continued to fill the void and its importance to me as the years went on.

All this to say, we have dreams, hopes, and aspirations that bend, mold, and shape by sometimes the wisp of an idea, the planting of a seed, or the fickle finger of fate.

"A journey of a thousand miles begins with one step," so the Chinese proverb goes. Before that first step, however, having the intention of ending at a certain destination is important too. Because there are bound to be diversions along the way, keeping a distant goal to navigate toward will assist in keeping you on course a little better. From the flicker of a thought to the culmination of a dream, all along the way we keep a vision of what we think it would look like to have what we want. After all, being the best marksman in the world with no target to shoot at provides him with no advantage over any novice. The distinction here is that the marksman, when a target opportunity does present itself, will be able to meet the challenge of hitting it with relative surety. And targets do change. Hit or miss, a new one will present itself. There usually is no shortage of a target to shoot at. The idea is to be ready for it. When preparation meets opportunity, a high level of success is almost assured.

Practicing, rehearsing, studying, memorizing, and repetition are the pillars that will support any endeavors we choose to focus on. In the early part of life, where to direct our attention is usually controlled by the adults in our lives. We may do all those things without knowing exactly why or where it will benefit us and are told to just do and trust things will work out later. That's just fine if you know what you are training for. What if you have no idea what should be pursued? What direction should you even face? How do you know if you will be great at something or just even good? After acquiring all of these skills, maybe we still do not know how to start, almost like being at a buffet table. It all looks good, and you know you can't have it all, at least at this sitting. So what comes first?

My answer to those questions is typically, "You don't know until you attempt something." And it cannot be a half-hearted attempt. If, after you have given your all, you find it is not to your liking, then move on. But at least you have been exposed to it. Love it or leave it. If you love it, keep working. And then the opportunities may appear sooner than later.

Malvolio from Shakespeare's *Twelfth Night* said, "Some people are born great, some achieve greatness, and others have greatness thrust upon them."

Most of us end up doing what we do because we encounter forks in the road and we are presented with a choice. And so often, it wasn't much of a choice. It was thrust upon us. Or one outweighed any other. How wonderful it would be if our choices were always the result of our achievements. Even when encountering forks in the road by design, there is always room for the misstep leading us into new and different directions. Rarely do we get the chance to correct these diversions down a new road. But if we know the ultimate destination, we can usually get there by way of detour. Some would make the case it is the fortunate ones who can have the vision of such a planned out life. I suspect that, more times than not, when we get diverted for one reason or another (some call this life), our paths never quite bring us back to the original plan.

Then there are those who have no clue what direction to take in the long term and live by the adage, "If you don't know where you are going, any road will take you there."

My point is: We get to where we are going by different methods, influences, and events. Talents need cultivating, nurturing, and encouragement. Circumstances and timing are almost never lined up perfectly. A life's journey is transfigured by many, many factors. It would be simplistic of me to set it down to a handful or so reasons we do what we do and how we get to where we get. One thing is absolute. A map will do no good if we can't read it. Knowledge is essential and will be acquired along the way. Knowledge won't always prevent bad turns but can minimize the turnarounds or "the long way around scenic routes," as I call them. The map itself may be outdated and not even have the information on it yet, so there are many unpredicted obstacles to negotiate to boot. Once in a great while, we do chart a new, trouble-free course. That can be very exciting.

Look back in your own life, and you will quite likely see the places where the path divided and your choices in those moments took you away from where you originally intended.

The paths and roads that led me to this career manifested over time. With no grand scheme occurring from an early age, things slowly developed by trial and error. There seemed to be a lot of that. Who would set out to be a mime? This wasn't an ambition overriding all other ambitions. I did not set out to be an actor. There wasn't an inkling of a thought about it or even becoming a fine musician. Since knowing more about music, teaching music played a few thoughts.

Of course, no evidence of later being a stay-at-home full time dad, never mind the idea of being a dad in the first place, percolated in this head. The hats worn on this adventure, past the seen and unseen forks, getting to this point in my life depict who I am.

All that we say or do begins with a thought. The thought ruminates in our heads, and either it may remain a thought or we can give power to that thought by giving voice or action to it. Big or small, these thoughts move us in directions we hope will lead to good results.

As James Allen says in *As a Man Thinketh*, "Every thought-seed sown or allowed to fall into the mind, and to take root there, produces its own, blossoming sooner or later into act, and bearing its own fruitage of opportunity and circumstance. Good thoughts bear good fruit, bad thoughts bad fruit."

In the unraveling of my travels, the recurring theme of what I encounter in the lives of people is the want of a meaningful life, to be significant in some way and to have relevance and to make a positive impact on the world. The driving cause of this, I believe, is hope—hope to make a difference, to contribute, and to produce a meaningful life. Without hope, staying on the simple and easy course, not taking chances to better situations or, worse, giving up and letting life randomly happen, would ultimately leave me empty I feel.

Turning points can be identified with relative authority when looking back and knowing the outcome. What get lost over time are the extraneous circumstances that became part of the choosing process. Details, conditions, state of mind and relationships, goals and ambitions—all contributed to the direction that took place. In reflecting on these periods, bits and pieces of memories coalesce. Some are starkly vivid with some recollections jostled loose in the untangling. In the retelling, hopefully I will make good sense of the why, how, where, and who, to mold for you a solid image—more accurately, a tapestry woven, given substance and meaning by the lives I have touched and those who have touched mine.

At an early age, some people have the vision and clarity of what they want to do for the rest of their life. There are those who stay focused to achieve that. I marvel at that thought. The side of my brain that wants order and neatness, with everything in its place with predictable outcomes, has not developed strong enough to override appreciation for randomness. It must be admitted here that it is a battle at times, exacerbated by having a wife whose brain is wired for neatness and orderliness. She is a surgeon. In her world it is imperative to be orderly and disciplined. I am sure being left-handed has something to do with it, but cannot verify that because she can do things right-handed as well.

When it is revealed in conversation that I used to perform and am a mime, there is always a curiosity about it, almost a mystique that surrounds this information. The discovery of my being a mime seems to always come with eyebrows raised, head tilts, and mouths that form little o's. It is a unique profession to be sure. Maybe that is one of the reasons I enjoy it so much. To answer the question that is always posed, "So what do you do for a living?" with "I'm a mime" has almost always generated conversation. These conversations led to some very interesting chats most of the time. By merely admitting to be an actor and answering in that way, I am quite sure the reactions would not have been as entertaining.

Meeting people or students who had not been exposed to mime or pantomime occurred frequently. Explaining that pantomime is the art of acting using facial expressions and movement without the benefit of using language generally led to being asked to do at least a few mime moves such as pulling on a rope, making a wall, leaning on a shelf, or something small to demonstrate the agility of creating something out of thin air. Traditionally we are called pantomimes, a name which is actually the telling of stories without words but is used to describe us as well. A person who does pantomime is now just called a mime, for the most part, but both names are accurate and acceptable.

Having had to do so much self-promotion over the years, I relied on this ability to open up a conversation. This could present potential job opportunities. In an entertaining way, it helped me explore that potential. The end result would, hopefully, be that it would make meeting me stand out. I never knew the outcome of such an introduction. Who really does? Looks can be deceiving, and it served me well in listening more than talking. We all want to share who we are. We are usually very proud of what we do and like it when the conversation swerves into our interests. Along the way, one of the very memorable lessons that I learned is "If you want to be found interesting, be interested." For me, treating others with respect in all circumstances (unless remarkably provoked or unintentionally impolite) kept me from worrying about stepping on toes, and I learned about many people in the process.

It has been a blessing to have had so many opportunities to express myself. When measured against what is considered traditional success, artists sometimes question their value. I suppose most of us question our value from time to time.

This poem emanated from a reflection of my career to that point, writing this not to be boastful, but more as an affirmation and at the same time giving myself a bit of a pep talk. In case you ever wondered what a mime says in a self-talk session, this may give you a clue about what this mime reaffirmed.

I Am an Artist
Ken Alcorn (July 1986)

I am an artist.
I can write, and do.
I can act, and do.
I can sing, and do.
I can dance, and do.
I am an artist.
I can paint, and do.
I can compose, and do.
I can play piano, and do.
I can do mime, and do.
I am an artist.
I can create, perform, entertain, and do.
I can touch souls, share dreams, wax poetic, and do.
I can do these things, and do.
I can do these things well, and I do.
Making money? Well, not enough! Why?
I suppose because it is that I say,
I am an artist.
And because beauty and joy are taken for granted,
And self-expression is scrutinized and trampled upon,
And stifled by the masses who can't and don't,
An artist must create his statement for the love of his art,
And the satisfaction that a creation is personal
and maybe reflects humanity!
All this to only say,
I am an artist.
And sometimes I question the payoff.
And sometimes crave for an answer,

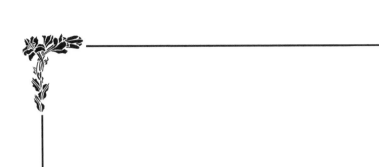

And sometimes just know exactly why,
And always too proud to give it up!
To glory in the realization, the honor
And announcement to the world that indeed,
I am an artist.
And this is a gift.

What would life be if we had no courage to attempt anything?

—Vincent Van Gogh

CHAPTER

2

When the Dream Took Root

My Family

Talent and individualism were nurtured in our family. My father, George, lived through the depression and lost his father at the young age of nine to an automobile accident, an irony because my grandfather never drove a car and sat as the passenger at the time. Dad being the youngest of five by a good many years stayed home with my grandmother until he went into the Air Force. My grandmother would take in boarders to help defray costs, a very common practice in those days. The National Bank of New Jersey (NBNJ) recruited Dad to work for them right out of high school. He left for his time in the service and then returned after it ended. He then pursued his Bachelor of Science degree from Rutgers University going to night school as our family grew. His banking career spanned forty-two years. A dream career for him, though, would have been as a singer with his beautiful bass voice, both speaking and singing. My mother, Jane, came from a family of seven children. She held the fifth position. Mom met Dad while going into the NBNJ where Dad by now had worked his way up to teller after starting in the mail room. He didn't stand a chance. It was game, set and match. Mom made her choice as Dad very quickly found out. They married and had six children, of which I am third in line. My mother would have been a wonderful dancer. She had the beauty of a model but not the height.

Her soprano voice also would have made her a force had she been able to pursue that. In her family, these attributes were appreciated but not cultivated. This too, I believe, was the result of the Great Depression where practicality reigned over desire.

All of my siblings are abundantly talented. My oldest sister, Linda, a mother of two boys, has a wonderful singing voice and sang with The Sweet Adelines, an a cappella chorus, but really shone in her barbershop quartet, in which she performed for many years. My older brother, Bob, is a commercial artist and father of two girls and has had an extraordinary career in painting. He also can sing and was recruited multiple times for the Broadway musical *Grease* back in the 1970s and turned it down each time. He felt uncomfortable on the stage, so he stuck with painting. And he had married his high school sweetheart Kathy, also an artist. His artwork made it to the covers of *Newsweek* and *Time* magazines, brochures for NASA, album covers, theater posters, and commercial accounts too numerous to mention. One of my favorite stories revolves around one piece of art he designed and painted for the Bloomingdale's Christmas shopping bag. It depicted Santa Claus in a spacesuit flying through space carrying a Bloomingdale's shopping bag full of toys and goodies.

I commuted to New York City for a short while. To catch the bus home at the Port Authority, I typically entered from 8th Avenue to the escalators taking me to the second floor usually grabbing a candy bar and a newspaper from the newsstand at the top of the escalator stairs for the hour ride home.

This one particular late afternoon, I stood next to a finely dressed woman, and quite beautiful, it might be added, as we rode up the escalator stairs. At the end of her hand, I noticed she carried one of the Bloomingdale's Christmas shopping bags that my brother had designed. She too stopped at the newsstand, and as we waited to pay for our papers, I pointed to the bag which separated us and casually mentioned that my brother was the artist who designed the Santa Claus bag she held. She turned her head to the left to look at me, not moving any other thing, tilted her head back, and then lifted her free hand to raise her sunglasses up without letting go of them, just enough to see I was clad in jeans and a simple jacket lugging a leather shoulder bag. She lifted the Bloomie's bag, gave it a quick glance, then returned her gaze to meet my eyes, and said in a matter-of-fact way, "You're full of **it!" Simultaneously, she dropped her bag back down to the toting position and then, in what seemed like three seconds, replaced her glasses, turned her head back forward, picked up a paper, placed her dollar on the remaining stack of papers, and disappeared forever into the crowd.

There is no question she thought it as a pickup line from some schlep in the bus station, though I didn't think of that at the time. In reality I was just proud of my brother and bragging about him. After being shot down, I laughed to myself all the way home in anticipation of going over to tell Bob what had happened.

He burst out laughing and, in a big brother fashion, asked me why I would say something like that. Didn't I know she would think it was a big come-on? Her response is now folklore between Bob and me. At appropriate moments, when that phrase can be plugged in, we'll unleash it and have another laugh. Those four words will retell the entire story, and the images are relived in a matter of moments. Bob has always done what he could to help me with getting my promotional material looking good.

Then came three younger sisters. Janice, a mother of four, has a tremendous gift of interior design. Actually, all of my sisters have. Janice loves to sing as well and has utilized her talents in praise worship. Beverly, a mother of two talented musicians, is the most naturally talented one of us all, in my opinion. She had done some theater and four musicals in high school as well as chorus and band, but later got married and had children. She also sings in a praise worship team and certainly has the heart of an artist. Melissa, my youngest sister, a mother of three boys, besides possessing many other gifts, is a remarkable comic. Her timing is impeccable, and her wit is razor-sharp. She had no interest in performing to my knowledge but had dreamed of being a comedy writer. Getting married right out of high school to her high school sweetheart John and having a family changed her focus. Nonetheless, we ache from laughter when we all get together. We'll even laugh when someone says things that aren't funny, laughing all the harder because it bombed.

There are successful talented artists, writers, photographers, jewelry designers, and musicians up and down both sides of the family tree. Having support from my parents or for us to encourage the arts for our children came quite naturally and expectedly.

Giving you a little background to my family will hopefully let you see that no matter what direction I went, it would be supported in spirit by the family. It is still this way today.

> Cherish your visions; cherish your ideals; cherish the music that stirs in your heart, the beauty that forms in your mind, the loveliness that drapes your purest thoughts, for out of them will grow all delightful conditions, all heavenly environment; of these, if you but remain true to them, your world will at last be built... Dream lofty dreams, and as you dream, so shall you become. (James Allen, *As a Man Thinketh*)

Am I Really That Different?

There are voices in my head that, when it is very quiet and I'm trying to fall asleep, sometimes even fully awake, talk. It is not all of the time, just occasionally, and usually when there is no real outside noise to drown them out. Not knowing if they are talking to me or with each other, it has become a challenge to identify them. Is this a normal occurrence? Do voices bounce around in everyone's heads? Are people, here and beyond, living or dead, trying to communicate with me but I'm merely limited in my comprehending and deciphering the messages, if they are even messages? Am I being guided in any way from them? Am I making too much of this and is this normal? Or is it only me working out a course of action for myself? Or is it the voice of God? After all, I would like to hear from Him.

Then there are the visions. I notice them when going to sleep or in a half sleep or the waking up process. They appear focused and vivid in the distance. And they appear in the very center of my view, seemingly far off with a deep and crystal clarity. Whatever I seem to be seeing, it is as though looking through an opening of a cloud, misty along the inner part of the tunnel shape that surrounds my vision (mind you my eyes are shut), most of the time not remembering much of the dream or vision or voices or even what it means but knowing they are there and were there.

My very favorite, of the ones keenly recalled, is when I can fly. This one is recurring. There are tall pillars surrounding a courtyard, and I can leap to the top of one from the ground and then jump down and swoop up to the top of any of the other columns. Launching from there to soar over the countryside for long distances it seems. It is a very free feeling and extraordinarily real and not dreamlike at all. When it slowly fades away, there is a tremendous feeling that this resides in truth and not imaginations or dreams, but realization takes hold that I'm not capable to do this same gliding on the totally conscious level. I have tried. It hasn't worked yet.

One night I dreamed about Fred Astaire. We were in a theater rehearsing on a thrust stage. The edge of the stage stood only a foot and a half high off the house floor. A thrust stage is one that reaches out into the audience unlike a proscenium arch stage that one thinks of traditionally when thinking of a theater. Fred was teaching me a specific dance routine when a delivery person or janitor came down the aisle and placed a bag of potatoes on the edge of the stage with a clock. Mr. Astaire and I said our goodbyes with a hug as he left me on the stage to practice the steps. It seems like a typical disjointed dream sequence, doesn't it? When I turned on the television that morning after waking up, it was reported that Fred Astaire had passed away during the night. This was June 22, 1987. I had never met him personally. He lived in California, while I lived in Virginia. Grabbing a notebook, I penned my dream and his reported death that very moment.

On another occasion, also while living in Northern Virginia on a farm in a barn that had a finished upstairs apartment, our bedroom windows faced north with Mount Weather in the distance over the hills. One evening around 9:00 p.m., with a now very dark, clear, and starry sky, my then wife and I happened to be talking while stretched crossways on the bed, gazing out the window, when a light from a flying object hovered what we perceived to be about a mile or so near the hilltops in the distance and then zipped in different directions at different speeds, stopping and starting and covering a large area, up and down, quickly and slowly off in the distance above Mount Weather. Mount Weather is a government facility that is built into the mountain and is a safe haven for government officials in the case of a threat to them in Washington, D.C. It is located about fifty miles to the west of the capital. We were on a farm, and visibility was quite broad above the Blue Ridge Mountains. We watched this for about twenty minutes before it took off, and the event ended. We were and I am certain it was a UFO. There were two of us who saw this, and we considered the possibility the lights could be helicopters or something of that nature. Nothing that zipped with that kind of speed and reversal of directions and the distances it covered in the time span of a second or two existed in our technology, to my knowledge. Our only regret is that we did not have a movie camera to record the happening.

In reality, these things give me no extra insight that I am aware of anyway. What does it all mean? I suspect only that there are unexplained occurrences in our lives that don't always have an explanation that fits neatly inside general perceptions. And whether this makes me outside the norm I couldn't tell you.

These things are mentioned to say that it has always seemed a possibility that what could not be seen or explained does not mean they do not exist. I am a mime and create illusions from nothing. It is how my mind is wired. Coming from the belief that God is omnipotent and has always existed, it made perfect sense to me that He could create something from nothing. Of my favorite quotes from the Bible, two that top that list are Hebrews 11:1, *Faith is the substance of things hoped for, the evidence of things not seen*, and 2 Corinthians 4:18, *While we look not at the things which are seen, but at the things which are not seen: for the things which are seen are tem-*

poral; but the things which are not seen are eternal. These two verses alone stand in direct opposition to our base understanding and how most go through life, taking the obvious and tangible as all there is.

Are there areas of skepticism? It's probably more of wondering how all of it fits, but my belief in God and what He can do and has done is not in doubt for me. I know He created each of us with our own gifts and talents, but from an early age felt different from most, not privileged or special or better in any particular way, just unique. And I am quite sure that most feel this way about themselves. Harboring this feeling of uniqueness from early in life I found expression learning and playing the piano, writing music, and poetry then through theater and eventually through mime.

Acting on the initial thoughts experienced as a youngster that I would stand out in a way that separated me from others has proved to verify, at least to me, that indeed we reap what we sow. How it manifests comes by way of thousands and thousands of little thoughts and actions, almost like a sculptor with bits of clay he adds or takes away or a painter by the paint strokes and color he applies to eventually bring the creation into existence. And the integrity in which those thoughts are directed determines the subsequent quality of the result. Or to say it another way, clarity of purpose sets in motion the course, but the quality of thought backed by proper action determines its excellence.

So where do we find these thoughts? Where do they come from? Are they our own, or are they floating around in some cosmic cloud waiting to be plucked? How do we explain multiple manifestations of the same ideas at almost the same time? Are they ideas whose time has come? Or, again, is it God speaking in that quiet voice?

Problems create a pull and demand for a solution. If there is enough energy surrounding a particular problem, solving it is only a matter of time.

What has gone before acts as a catalyst for more ideas and new thought. I found that this is true in the direction my life took and why. It can be traced back to earlier times where some of those thoughts and ideas, dreams, and hopes came from. Some remained dormant until more energy was spent working on the implementation of a solution.

> The vision that you glorify in your mind, the ideal that you enthrone in your heart—this you will build your life by, this you will become.
> (James Allen, *As a Man Thinketh*)

Influences

Many famous people influenced me. By watching entertainers like Harpo and Chico Marx (I did not really quite get the silliness of Groucho until much later), Red Skelton, Danny Kaye, Laurel and Hardy, The Three Stooges, Abbott and Costello, Buster Keaton, Charlie Chaplin, and Marcel Marceau, their impact on me came because they captivated and fascinated me.

Harpo showed me that disconnected things and having a different or skewed view of the world could be alright. He made me laugh harder than any of the others. Yet he displayed the certain seriousness when he played his harp. Chico intrigued me, from his Italian accent to the ease and panache of his piano playing making difficult appear simple.

Red Skelton made me giggle. Silliness and happiness danced around his characters, and even if I did not understand the jokes in my earlier years, he provided enough visuals to keep me watching becoming a ritual to stay up for his show on Tuesday nights at 8:30 p.m. My parents allowed this, though my bedtime was 8:00 p.m. typically, with them seeing how much of a kick I got from him. Only years later would I discover the larger body of work he produced as a movie actor and where he emitted his gentle charm and affability in most all he did.

Danny Kaye stood above most all others in my eyes, an enormous talent who taught me to use my entire body in movement and my face in expression. To me he exuded musicality making everything he did, also as with the others mentioned, look effortless and flowing. His patter songs were remarkable and still are to this day. His timing in everything he portrayed seemed to me to be perfection. Being serious or goofy or anything that the moment called for, Danny Kaye struck a chord with me. The news of his death saddened me greatly, and while living on a farm in the country in Northern Virginia, tears formed and fell as I worked a rake around our yard. Isn't it interesting how certain people or things affect us?

Laurel and Hardy, like Abbott and Costello and The Three Stooges, were fun because of the situations they created and the sight gags that pointed up the ridiculous. I preferred Stan Laurel over Oliver Hardy and Curly of The Three Stooges more than all the others who tried to fill his role, from Shemp to Joe Besser to Curly Joe. Larry always stuck in the middle evoked a bit of sympathy from me. Moe smothered Larry, where he remained forevermore the abiding scapegoat. Because of Moe's meanness, I cheered against him probably since he held the dominant position. But giving Moe his due credit, he truly mastered his craft. And who could not side with Lou Costello over the slick, manipulative, and conniving Bud Abbott? I have an older brother. If you analyze this, it could explain my gravitating to those characters and probably why I identified with "The Beaver" on the TV show *Leave It to Beaver* (though a few of my friends thought I came off more like Eddie Haskell, the epitome of a suck-up around their parents; I was simply being polite). My brother and "Wally" were cut from the same cloth it seemed.

Buster Keaton, Charlie Chaplin, and Harold Lloyd all influenced me much later admiring and appreciating their craft as they worked it. I do not remember them so much as a youngster.

If you wish to glimpse inside a human soul and get to know a man, don't bother analyzing his ways of being silent, of talking, of weeping, of seeing how much he is moved by noble ideas; you will get better results if you just watch him laugh. If he laughs well, he is a good man. (Fyodor Dostoyevsky)

Hightstown High School (HHS) Days

"Of all the words of tongue or pen, the saddest
are these: It might have been."

—John Greenleaf Whittier

Along with the eighth grade diploma, each student received the book *The Great State Papers of New Jersey*. Instead of a yearbook, which did not exist for our eighth grade, we passed this book around for students and teachers to sign saying "Good luck in high school," "Wishing you well in the future," and "Always stay the same" type of messages that could be read years later for a bit of a memory jog taking us back to a period of time possibly tucked away in the recesses of our minds. And sometimes there are messages that are remembered because they struck a chord. In this case, *The Great State Papers of New Jersey* with the classmates' and teachers' inclusions serves as my example of this.

There is a quote from one of my teachers that made an impact on me throughout my life. My book is packed away somewhere, and I haven't seen it for years. But his comment is as fresh today in my mind as the day it was written and read by me, a long, long time ago. You just read it. It is the John Greenleaf Whittier quote. My teacher penned this to me and hoped I "would not be using this quote in the near future. Wise up!" I have found it interesting that this still, even as I write this, brings about an emotional response. I am at once both incensed by the comment and thankful—incensed because it was accurate and shot an arrow right through my ego and thankful because it influenced my life and although appearing a bit harsh and possibly flippant, it has caused me to think about it on many levels ever since. This warning came from my geography teacher, and though not being a miserable student, you would recognize a very serious student elsewhere, especially in classes that didn't quite inspire me. That never really changed much until maturity tried to take over and I made the choice to buckle down and it became necessary to take my future seriously, a good seven years after this seemingly perspicacious note. It's not that I hadn't been searching for the opportunity. It seemed like an opportunity was all I tried to find, eluding me until a level of confidence and a small degree of wisdom developed enough to pull things together. This took me a while. (As a matter of fact, I think sometimes there are those that might still be waiting for me.)

A person's lasting impression isn't always predictable. All the while that quote sat in my head. Russell Wilbur could never have known the impact of his written entry in that graduation gift book and have often wondered why he wrote that to me. The fascinating thing is he probably wouldn't remember this in the least. Why should he? Obviously, he saw something in me that I had not recognized myself. And what he observed in me as possibly a lack of seriousness I had, even at that time, was the soul of an artist trying to find my expression.

Upon entering high school, theater and anything related to the stage had not crossed my mind. That direction did not present itself just yet. My older brother and sister had already paved the way into high school. Now being the third Alcorn to walk the halls of Hightstown High School, I ran for class president and won. Serving on the student council along with my older brother, Bob, made high school a less fearful place I thought. Trying to carve my own way with a brother striding the halls as the worldly senior and the still fresh memory of my older sister Linda's presence, having graduated two years before, I perceived to be off to a good start. If people did not know me, they knew of me. There were eleven hundred students or so. Just joining the band and choir exposed me to one quarter of the school. Linda's beauty quickly drew attention, and Bob had this ubiquitous way about him. They set the stage, and I made the entrance. Living in the neighborhood of the high school made it very easy to spend a lot of extra time getting involved with after-school activities without the need for a ride. Choosing soccer as my sport because my mother would not let me try out for the football team probably saved my life. I would have been killed. Still waiting for a growth spurt being an average runner and being asthmatic were not a particularly winning combination for a career in sports. It did not stop me from playing soccer either, but I played goalie so I did not have to run up and down the field as much. That triggered the asthma, but I figured if I kept running, it might make me stronger—mind over matter. My parents, in trying to protect me from getting hurt, said no to my playing football. They did not realize how a goalie protecting the soccer net faced potentially more devastating treatment at the hands of an opponent. They only knew there weren't as many collisions in soccer, but with no pads or helmet, the risk posed as much of a threat to my body. So I played soccer in the fall in position of goalkeeper. Playing with abandon and no fear translated into a pretty good season. I rarely got scored upon and never got hurt as it turned out.

The soccer coach also coached the gymnastics team. He encouraged me, so I joined the team. We were not very good, though there were some outstanding gymnasts. But I did earn my first varsity letter. The point system that the coach used determined who would qualify for a letter, with me scoring enough to get my big H, vaulting the long horse.

My first competition was memorable. First touching my toes, I prepared for the running approach by stretching my arms out to the side like an angel stretches his wings. My arms fell back down to my side, and then with a starting burst of speed, they pumped with each passing step, darting down the approach strip toward the looming long horse that needed vaulting. Calculating every aspect of this maneuver, I leaped at full tilt, pouncing on the sweet spot of the springboard with every intention of propelling up, up, and over the apparatus to the desired perfectly stuck landing. I instead managed a line drive trajectory launching myself squarely onto the end of the horse causing an abrupt and instant stop to my torso while my arms, legs, and head continued on in rag doll appearance. Thump! The horse and I were now one with me being almost impaled on the front end of the apparatus. Instantly, a collective gasp from the spectators filled the gymnasium, then followed by silence as I gently melted off the end of the horse. My stomach and hips took the impact of what the entire viewing crowd had thought to be my subsequent debut as a soprano. It must have looked brutal. A mass sigh of relief and a polite applause to cover up what everyone was thinking spread though the bleachers. This would probably go viral on YouTube nowadays. My brother still ribs me about that one. By the way, I cleared the horse on my second run and earned a 4.1 score out of 10 (not very respectable). Compared to the first jump, a champion probably couldn't have felt better though getting over the thing might have been my only real accomplishment that day, surviving ranked right up there too. Improvement came as the year went on but not very much. My tumbling pretty much matched my long horse skills. The school cut gymnastics out of the sports roster the following year replacing it with wrestling, but trying it for one week, it reminded me of my younger days wrestling my brother. I really did not like it then either. He would pin my arms down as he sat on me and twiddle the inside of my nostril with a blade of grass or quickly run a comb edgewise just below my nose. Yes, Bob, I remember! Anyway, wrestling held no interest.

About this time came the announcement for the musical auditions. Theater now loomed on the horizon. Going back a little, shortly after moving to Hightstown, New Jersey, from Milltown, in junior high school, I joined the band choosing to play the tuba or sousaphone. My folks had given me a season of drum lessons in sixth grade before the move. That gave no satisfaction because I never hit a drum having only been given one of those little six-by-five-foot rubber and wood drum pads that went dink-dink-dink-dinka-dinka-dink when you hit it, with amazingly, real drumsticks. This sure felt like the accordion or piano bait-and-switch routine all over again. Lucy holding the football for Charlie Brown came to mind.

The looks I absorbed from passersby while walking the mile home with the sousaphone on my shoulder were pretty funny, especially exiting the shortcut through the town's graveyard on the way home. I turned more than a few heads. I considered carrying a tuba on my shoulder all the way home remarkably cool and certainly looked better than trying to push a piano down the street or playing my little rubber drum pad going dink-dink-dinka-dink the whole mile trek. There were days, though, that I wished I picked the trumpet. I started piano lessons at five years old on the promise of learning the accordion later, as mentioned earlier. The opportunity for the accordion never materialized, so the piano prevailed. There seemed a natural gravitation to music in high school where I joined the band and, of course, marched the sousaphone on game day Saturdays.

The lure of a finely trimmed uniform certainly wasn't the reason I joined the band. In my freshman year, the band wore white pants and shoes, with a white shirt and a blue blazer, which we all had to provide. That made up our uniform. We sold candy and Christmas cards and had all kinds of fund-raisers to earn our uniforms for my sophomore year. They were sharp-looking, deep royal-blue suits with white-, silver-, and blue-trimmed overlays, on which HHS was emblazoned on the front for Hightstown High School and on the back was a ram head. We were the Rams. We wore white spats along with blue fuzzy helmets in the tradition of the English guards.

Our band director, exuded passion for music. Known for his remarkable Irish wit, he could be stern too. Although he laughed and found humor in most things, when we needed to work, we knew it. He instilled pride in our band, and although the football team wasn't very good most of my years there, the band carried the banner of pride to every event we played. We covered the field, marching over 120 instruments. In this era at Hightstown High, we considered it an honor to belong to the band, and we believed it. At least I did. Many of us spent a lot of time in the band and choir rooms during high school, conveniently located across the hall from the auditorium backstage area, another favorite place to hide from classes while doing something important like setting the lights, sweeping the stage, or rearranging the wings. If you were to ask me to draw the layout of that part of the building, to this day, I could get it very close, unlike my trying to draw the science wing of the school.

My sister Beverly, who a few years later would star in *Guys and Dolls* playing Adelaide (absolutely tremendous in that role), reminded me how our band director would have us doing the polka through the band room, out and down the hall and then back into the other door completing the circle. Once she told me of that, I also remembered he did the same thing with us with the waltz, because we needed to waltz in *My Fair Lady*. He loved to roller-skate, so,

41

for fun, he would take us on roller-skating trips to a roller rink in South Amboy.

Playing the piano provided a new way of making money, once I got my driver's license. Since I played the old standards from the 1930s, 1940s, 1950s, and 1960s, cocktail piano as it is called, there were occasional opportunities to make money. One of my very first piano playing gigs took place in a New Year's Eve party for the local police at The Cranbury Golf Clubhouse called The Bog, which laid the foundation for me to later play in restaurants, hotels, inns, weddings, business dinners, and events such as these.

Back in the spring of my freshman year, the school put on the musical *Oliver*. My brother, Bob, a senior, played a supporting role in it. I came away thinking it would be fun to be on stage. He hated the stage as I found out, suffering from a bit of stage fright. It is something that I have never feared or suffered from. In the spring of my sophomore year, we put on *The Music Man*. In my junior year, we produced *My Fair Lady*. I played Harry, one of Alfie P. Doolittle's drinking buddies, and sang bass in the quartet.

During my senior year, I landed the part of George Gibbs in *Our Town* in the fall. Now in rehearsals for the show and on an off day for me, on this extremely rainy autumn day, I traveled down Route 130 near Dayton, New Jersey, in the family Volkswagen van on the way to my orthodontic appointment. Traveling about forty-five miles per hour, not really a high rate of speed but just enough to cause me to hydroplane, the water built up between the tires and the pavement preventing me from controlling the now swerving car, gliding between the two lanes heading north and then spinning two-and-a-half times when the van hit sideways onto the median causing it to flip over a couple of times and ending on its side facing the oncoming traffic heading south in the fast lane of the highway. Fortunately, the tractor trailer heading toward me traveling on an uphill grade had plenty of time to stop. A few people came to my assistance to help me out. I must have been in shock, because when people asked my name, I replied, "George Gibbs." My mother remembered that a minister came to my aid and asked me that question. Seat belts were still optional at the time, so buckling up wasn't an automatic thing as it is today. I remember holding onto the steering wheel while flipping going over. As the car lay on its side, I casually walked out the back hatch door. The van ended up totaled, yet I walked away unscathed, fortunately.

When spring came around, the part of Cornelius Hackl in *Hello, Dolly!* became my newest challenge. On the Friday night about a week before the show was to open, a few of us got hold of some Boone's Farm Strawberry Hill wine and a bottle of Southern Comfort. We drank too much, illegally I must tell you, leaving us all very, very hung over for play practice on the following Saturday morning. Word got around to the director of our condition, if it wasn't evident anyway. Art Neill played Mr. Vandergelder, the grocery store owner, and did not participate in the prior evening's party with Frank Smith playing Barnaby, Cornelius's friend, who did. Frank and I were feeling quite miserable. When we got to the scene where Mr. Vandergelder stomped heavily on top of the trapdoor for Barnaby and Cornelius, who were crouching below ready to pop out, it was then that the director exacted his brutal wit. With each stomp that came crashing down, only inches above our heads, Frank and I winced in pain from the continual pounding. As we emerged from the small confines of the set below the trapdoor, the director would yell from the auditorium, "Stop! Do it again. You were too slow!" He must have done this at least a dozen times. Unbeknownst to us, he instructed Art to stomp as hard as possible. The director never said a word to us about it. The entire cast stood around laughing watching our misery. I can tell you I still remember how good lunch tasted that day. Even now, I do not think many hamburgers have ever tasted that good. Maybe part of the relishing was because we had a break and a chance to recover. Our musical did turn out to be a great production in spite of our foolishness. After this show, I started to think theater might be my calling.

Shawnee on Delaware

My older brother and sister, Bob and Linda, became friends with Craig and Jo D Sechler in high school. Craig happened to be one of the really good gymnasts on our team, so I knew him pretty well too. Their father, Clyde, worked as a musical director for Fred Waring, founder of Fred Waring and The Pennsylvanians, a large, nationally well-known traveling chorus in the same vein as Lawrence Welk. For a period of time, Clyde directed a local variety show, and my family became involved with it. They were top-notch productions with professionals mixed in with the local talent. Auditions were held to be cast in the show. The piano accompanist, Norm Snell, played with the jazz drummer, the great Gene Krupa. I took lessons from Norm for five years. Each year Fred Waring hosted a summer intensive workshop for aspiring singers and musicians with a live performance at the end at his headquarters at Shawnee on Delaware. The summer after graduating high school, Clyde invited me to attend. This experience expanded my understanding of a bigger world out there.

A few years later, in another musical revue in Princeton, I sang "Mama, A Rainbow" from *Minnie's Boys*, a musical about the Marx brothers. This evolved directly from my experience at the McCarter Theatre after being in the cast of the musical *Carousel*.

He who has imagination without learning has wings and no feet.

—Joseph Joubert

CHAPTER

3

COLLEGE YEARS

Mercer County Community College (MCCC)

Partly because I was awarded a $200.00 scholarship for college from the band, music appeared to be the logical choice for a major. The scholarship money covered my first semester of college tuition, which when considering the costs of college now is amazing. (Of course inflation over that time made it appear that there was a huge disparity. Gasoline back then went for around $.22 a gallon, candy bars $.10, bread around $.25 a loaf, and cigarettes about $.38 a pack; so things seem about ten times the cost now, but taxes have added to some of those products.) While attending Mercer County Community College in Trenton, New Jersey, theater pulled me to my future; and in the first semester in college, my name appeared on the cast list for Tennessee Williams's *Camino Real* directed by Michael Mathias and understudy for the lead Kilroy along with my playing in the ensemble. During rehearsals there always seemed to be someone missing, so I usually filled in all the missing parts eventually learning all of the lines to the play like this. And it turned out well for me. The lead actor playing Kilroy broke his nose in a fraternity football game a week before the opening and could not perform. Because of his misfortune, I took over the lead and slipped in without missing a beat. Although on the avant-garde side of theater it was very well received, the adage of "when preparedness meets opportunity" aptly fit the situation.

This directly led to my getting the lead of Jerry in Edward Albee's *The Zoo Story*. It is a two-character play. My college history professor, David Collier, played the other part. David gave me so much to work off of. Through the thirteen-page monologue that Jerry delivered, his facial expressions drove me to keep it going. He later told me he only reacted to what I was doing as if it were the first time he had heard it.

Just down the street from the New Jersey State Capital building, MCCC scheduled a theater festival in the Hotel Hildebrecht ballroom on State Street, Trenton. Mercer County Community College utilized it before the new campus in West Windsor became its home. All classes in the downtown Trenton buildings and all the theater rehearsals and shows were held in the hotel ballroom that year. Opulence had long removed itself from this now dark, dingy, and dusty old hotel. Traces of its beauty remained but not evident anymore. The ballroom, with its vaulted ceiling and its massive columns, must have been extremely lovely until it fell to neglect, but now provided a great place for theater with its interesting space.

The lineup of the plays on the day of the festival had *The Zoo Story* in second position, followed by *Antigone's Wedding*, directed by Michael Mathias, the director from *Camino Real* and, by the way, the head of the theater department. I had been made aware in the rehearsal period that apparently there had been a battle to recruit me for their production, but Mathias did not get to me in time when I agreed to *The Zoo Story*. So with all of my family and guests ready for my performance already seated, with me already in makeup and ready to perform, Michael changed the order of the performances for some reason with *The Zoo Story* now to follow *Antigone's Wedding*. News of the schedule shift reached backstage. When viewing that the stage, a circle in the round affair, had indeed been set up for the other show, I seethed.

Bolting out to the center of the performance space, in front of the now seated audience, I confronted Mathias, perched in his seat on the top row of the platform in a very obvious location, and stated that we were about to perform *The Zoo Story*. He looked shocked that anyone would oppose him so boldly and openly. Maybe this boldness came from already being in character for the performance. From that point the audience witnessed, in very fast order, the blur of me moving his set pieces off the stage to set up the lone bench in the center of the stage for our performance. Mathias sat on his pudgy hands observing dumbstruck and fixed to his chair, like a stone Buddha.

With all the authority I could muster, I proclaimed to the audience "Ladies" and glared directly at Mathias when saying, "and gentlemen," before including the wide-eyed, stock-still patrons in continuing with "we will now present Edward Albee's *The Zoo Story* followed by *Antigone's Wedding* as listed in the program."

Leaving the stage for an extended moment to break the friction, ever so subtly, we immediately reentered and took our places to begin the play. David gave me an approving head nod just before we turned around to enter, as if to say, "Good job!" David would not have butted heads with his colleague as I had just done, but it upset him to be put in that position by Mathias. He would later confide. That is why he gave me that look. It turned into one of my most intense performances I ever have performed. That episode just primed my pump and added a layer to an already complicated role. At first the audience thought this was all part of the production. Later, after the show, the truth came out that this had transpired as a retribution for my not taking the other play, meant to humiliate me, to embarrass me. I stood my ground for what I believed fair. So, in this instance, his ploy backfired. David appreciated that I fought for us.

To this day my parents continue to hold that pre-show stance as a defining moment in my life. They have said it was a courageous thing to do, that it instilled a certain feeling of pride in my showing no fear in that situation, to stand up to an injustice and power play, to take action, to remain in control, and then to actually deliver a performance that they deemed remarkable. I hold it to be one of my most memorable experiences. Making my parents proud on top of that added to the day. And after all, isn't that what we hope for, if not overtly but at the base? But to be clear, I sought only to perform what and when it had been arranged. Being already mentally set, made up, and ready to perform and then to be pushed out of our spot at the last moment was wrong. Had we been informed before the festival began, I am quite sure we would have obliged with no resistance. Seeking out a confrontation without provocation is not something I do, but I will stand firm if circumstances necessitate. For the most part, I tend to be very amenable and flexible in most situations.

That festival turned out to be the last performances ever given there. With the new campus in West Windsor, New Jersey, came the brand-new Kelsey Theatre, a beautiful little theater with a thrust stage that sat at ground level with seating fanning out and up at a capacity of about 350. The opening two shows for the theater in the fall and winter saw me cast in the starring role in the opening show, a musical *Oh! What a Lovely War* set in the World War I era, and as the tavern owner in the next production, *The Tavern*, for which I later received the Outstanding Actor Award from MCCC that year. But because no one mentioned that there could be a chance I'd be awarded this honor, I didn't arrange to be at the ceremony instead of playing in a fraternity baseball game going on at the same time outside. I had no inkling about an award. Bill Flynn, the drama professor and director, presented me with the award later though a bit upset with me. He had never mentioned the importance for me to be there. I actually didn't realize the awards ceremony to be a big deal, never really ever having received an award before. The disappointment on his face, as I apologized for the apparent slight, was evident.

"Honors don't happen every day in this business," Bill would say to me. "It's important to recognize that."

How true that is. A lesson like that is sometimes learned the hard way. My fraternity brothers have long since diminished in any relevance to my life, and I couldn't tell you if that unimportant baseball game was won or lost.

The American Academy of Dramatic Arts (AADA), New York

After three semesters at MCCC, I applied to the American Academy of Dramatic Arts in New York City and received my first formal training in theater and mime. The mime classes were taught by Rudy Benda and Doug Day, also members of the Claude Kipnis Mime Troupe. Claude came in and gave master classes from time to time. They taught the basics of mime here. Mime is just one tool in the actor's toolkit. Little did I know that this was where the mime seed started its germination! We also studied period and style, exploring different eras and the mannerisms that were prevalent in those times. Jazz, tap, and ballet were also taught. Voice and speech, diction, accents, and projection were heavily covered. Performance and script analysis and improvisation classes were added to the curriculum.

One benefit of being in New York is that it allowed me to see Broadway shows pretty frequently. Tickets were made available at a huge discount provided to the school and also TKTS, a discount ticket outlet in the middle of Times Square. Another plus was that you could get a seven-ounce draft beer at The Blarney Stone (chain of bars) for a quarter.

Special guest lecturers would come in from time to time. Tommy Tune, starring on Broadway in *Seesaw* at the time, sat down with us to give a talk. Him being six feet six and very thin and his tap dancing in clogs made for a very unique and memorable visage. He spoke about the show and the business in general. Mr. Tune produced, directed, choreographed, and starred on Broadway for many years to come.

Raising my hand, I asked him, "Do you ever get the urge to spontaneously dance?"

He said, "Sometimes!"

I then asked, "Do you feel that urge coming on now?"

Everyone laughed, and he responded to me with "Who planted you in the audience with that question?"

No one asked me to ask, but I later heard there was someone planted. I happened to beat them to the punch.

On another occasion, Dana Andrews spoke to us about his career dating back to the 1940s, with a steady career after that. Some will remember him now, but he starred in many movies back then. He served as president of the Screen Actors Guild (SAG) from 1963 to 1965 and spoke out against women having to degrade themselves to land a part in Hollywood. He also spoke in later years about the effects of alcoholism on his career. Being an alcoholic, he came to the conclusion it was a miserable way to live and quit. When I met him, only a year had passed after he had made one of the very first public service announcements on television about alcoholism awareness. Alzheimer's disease affected his final years. Burt Lancaster visited his dear friend regularly, and while visiting Mr. Andrews, Mr. Lancaster suffered a debilitating stroke from which he never recovered.

We also had the opportunity to meet Richard Rodgers of Rodgers and Hart and then later Rodgers and Hammerstein. These two partnerships are legendary. The impact of their music on the musical world is, to this day, remarkable. For me, a simple handshake and a few words provided a link to that part of the entertainment world and roots to musical theater history that I appreciate still. When he shook our hands, he said hello and asked each of us to name a song he wrote. When he got to me, I sang the first few bars of "My Funny Valentine." He nodded with a smile and said thank you.

The girl following me couldn't answer, and he gently said to her, "Oh, come now. I wrote nine hundred of them. Surely you know of one?"

And she answered with a questioning, "Oklahoma?"

"That's right. There you did it," he kindly said.

Isn't it great that successful artists would return back to inspire the aspiring group of actors? To me, this gave some insight to the history of the profession with a few personal experiences.

All these classes helped lay the groundwork for my future. I attended AADA for one year. It is a two-year program, and the second year is by invitation only. I did not get the invitation. Neither did Barbra Streisand when she attended.

By this time in my life, I had worked at about twenty different part-time jobs, from pumping gas at a station to unloading train cars, a salesman in a men's shop, multiple positions at a movie theater, cooking hamburgers at a golf club, selling advertising over the phone, pizza delivery in New York City, modeling, newspaper boy, moving irrigation pipe on a farm, construction, digging ditches with an excavating business, bellhop, shoveling snow, waiting tables at a convalescent home, teaching tennis, being a counselor at a summer camp, and, of course, playing the piano. Then after working a few months making hoagies, I decided it best to return to Mercer County Community College for the spring semester for a fourth semester to finish my AA degree. I only needed a few more credits to do so. The setback to getting that degree was that a language course that spanned two semesters needed to be fulfilled.

German did not come easily to me, and to continue in that class would have proved fruitless, like the three years of French in junior and senior high then switching to two years of Spanish in high school. I just did not really grasp the languages. N'est pas? If speaking the languages eluded me, the classes benefited my accents and pronunciations, at least. Finishing four semesters at MCCC still left me short three credits for an AA degree, but still needing the full year of a language, night school was considered. Instead, a break from college sounded better.

This time away from school gave me a chance to do a lot of local theater and, fortunately, great parts. My first professional shows came at the Bucks County Playhouse in New Hope, Pennsylvania, just up the river from Trenton. Becoming a member of the Bucks County Playhouse Repertory Company resulted from me being cast in the part of Jabez Stone in *The Devil and Daniel Webster* and then in *Twelfth Night. Guys and Dolls* brought in the New York actors. As a nonunion talent, it paid $25.00 a week. We rehearsed for one week for a two-week run (my sister Beverly played, by far, a better Adelaide than the one we had in this show, although she wasn't bad). Getting a chance to work with professionals gave me a few insights as well as a solid credit on my resume too. Since being paid for acting in this show, I considered myself a professional actor from that point on—broke but professional!

Getting time off from working full-time making hoagies at Aljon's Sub Shops, a local chain fondly remembered now only by the older longtime locals, wasn't a problem. At that time, thoughts of buying into the franchise took a back seat. Making submarine sandwiches forever did not light my fire, yet it was a fine enough job that earned me money while I figured things out. Buying into a business seemed like a good option at the time though. My father advised against it wanting me to return to college. He planted that seed hoping for it to sprout and root.

Even not knowing which way to go just yet, it seemed like I was getting there in record time.

During this time, there were reviews in the papers for shows I had performed in: *1776* playing Richard Henry Lee, *West Side Story* as Riff, Charlie Brown in *You're a Good Man, Charlie Brown* (two different casts), and Harry in Sondheim's *Company*, naming a few. Rachel Dennison, a local newspaper theater reviewer, knew our family from the variety shows that Clyde Sechler produced which both our families were part of. Her daughter, Becky, had attended the North Carolina School of the Arts (NCSA) in Winston-Salem, North Carolina, and recommended to my parents that I apply. She thought highly of my potential and knew very well the quality NCSA presented. Because of this recommendation, it made sense to fill out the paperwork. Once accepted into NCSA School of Drama, resuming my college career turned out to be basically starting all over again, but that did not matter. My dad's planted seed had indeed rooted, and now a direction emerged to get my degree.

The North Carolina School of the Arts

The North Carolina School of the Arts is now known as the University of North Carolina School of the Arts (UNCSA). It had always been part of the UNC system. Now it has it formally in its title. For our mascot, we are known as the Pickles, and our motto is "Sling 'em by the warts!" Being an arts school, somehow it fits. I still think it is a better name than the Demon Deacons or the Blue Devils. The Tar Heels is strange too, but I sort of like that one. I guess it's the Ram in me.

Suddenly, Private First Pickle Alcorn reported for duty. The school rotated on a trimester schedule making the second trimester right after the New Year in 1976, my starting line after auditioning on December 12. Had I stayed on campus that day for another hour or two, news of my acceptance would have been discerned instead learning by letter on December 28 giving me only five days to get down to North Carolina from New Jersey for college. Those five days were a frenzied as they evoked nothing but a blur of running around.

Starting out as a freshman for the third time in my college career, the three years of college I had already attended added up to one trimester of credits eliminating virtually only math, history, and science courses and needing only to take two English classes with the rest of my schedule left open for studying drama.

And as described for the curriculum at the American Academy of Dramatic Arts, the classes were more of the same but being a little older and possibly wiser. I appreciated this new opportunity, knowing this to be the path that needed forging. This school, away from New York City, made it easier to stay focused on my objective.

Class size required it to be divided into two groups. We all took the same classes, just switched order. We had different plays or projects that allowed us to work with each other regardless of the class and were cast into parts performed throughout the trimesters.

Since arriving in the middle of the year, most of the casts were already set. It came as a surprise to me and others when they cast me in a lead male part in *A Taste of Honey* with the sophomore class. Performances were held in the black box theater across the street from the campus. Actually, this used to be an old church now transformed into a great theater space. Looking back, I marvel at the huge opportunity for me. Each new role reaffirmed my path.

UNCSA has different schools: the School of Drama, the School of Music, the School of Fine Arts, the School of Design and Production, the Film School, and the School of Dance. The year I started, *Fantasy Roulette*, a forty-five-minute production of hand-picked actors, dancers, musicians, and techies from across all of the schools, toured high schools across North Carolina to promote the school and hopefully inspire more North Carolina students to attend. Tony Walsh cast me in the second tour of the show, taking over the part that Terry Mann had done. Terry, a sophomore at the time, similarly was an older student to the grade level. He has since gone on to an extraordinarily successful career on Broadway.

It is my belief that my work in *A Taste of Honey* led to the faculty casting me to go on tour during my freshman year with the sophomores. I considered this a great bonus and a strong affirmation of me worthy and talented enough to represent the school in this fashion. The sophomores, in general, were a very loose and easy-going bunch of people, and I thought I fit pretty well with them. The faculty felt my class to be a seemingly more studious and serious group. I fit pretty well there too. We had a bit of odd, a bit of cerebral, and plenty of talent. Because of the school's size, we were familiar with a large percentage of the students. Predominantly though, we worked mostly within our class levels.

The School of the Arts is not an easy one to navigate through. It takes hard work and discipline. A student has to be invited back each year. That almost did not happen after my freshman year. Those two trimesters were rough, and my grades reflected that. It did not help to be laid up in bed for over a week with the flu and that the *Fantasy Roulette* tour causing a lot of missed classes. That missed time put me behind in some classes. Eventually I got beyond that, and things progressed, but not without some soul searching. Over the next summer, I resolved that I would do the necessary work to earn my degree.

There were fifty-three students, including me, who originated or joined in my class with only fifteen completing the program to earn the Bachelor of Fine Arts in Drama degree. It is a rigorous training program, taught by professionals in all the disciplines offered. This school, founded in 1963, did not have the reputation of Julliard or Carnegie Mellon or Yale just yet. But as each year passed, the impact UNCSA made on the arts world by its alumni helped forge a solid reputation across the country.

This fellow's wise enough to play the fool. (William Shakespeare)

Becoming a Complete Actor

In the beginning of my training, one of my instructors said, "It takes twenty years to become a great actor. What's your hurry?"

This evoked a response of light laughter from the class. But he was quite serious. He allowed that, yes, although there were talented young actors working and they would not reach their full potential until they had lived through many more experiences to draw upon than most had by the time they were twenty. So while a ballet dancer's career is just about over very early, it is the actors who will need to grow into their art, as well as the musicians.

Subtleties mark the performances of the great actors, the great musicians, the great writers, and the great artists and dancers. That is acquired by doing and living and practicing. One cannot draw upon something that is not within their realm of experience or imagination without them. That is not to deny that even imagination gives a certain level of experience. If you imagine something, you at least are giving thought to that something. Even that will give the essence of experience to a degree, if not a fully blossomed one. In some cases, that essence of a thing will do on the first layer, the beginning point. It is the richness of experience that provides the depth and color to give substance to the other layers. A writer does not write a paragraph with only one word. A painter uses a choice of color. A dancer doesn't just hop up and down. A musician does not blat out one note. And an actor does not merely recite lines. All utilize those tools that will allow them to create something beyond the simple word, the brush stroke or one color, one hop or one note, by using a mixture of all that is available to them.

Anyone watching the television reality shows that include auditions or competition requiring skills knows that just having a need to win is not enough. There has to be an innate talent and some kind of internal spark that slices through the barriers—what some call the "it" factor. That one element of someone's performance ability will even cover up or override a lack of talent. If there is no connection between the performer and the audience, you, as the audience, are left with a very unsatisfying experience. A person with extraordinary talent and no charisma will fade into the background quickly but may have the skills to keep working. Conversely, someone with charisma and little talent may attain the initial glory of attention but usually cannot sustain that momentum. Of course, there are those with neither who somehow become sensations and last beyond their talent. Their timing happened to be right, and whatever they had to offer fit into perfect timing for them.

The purpose of training, in any profession, is to be able to do the job. Some will do better because of the experiences that they bring to it and, thus, launch from a higher platform. That does not mean that that position will always provide the advantage. Much of art and entertainment is a matter of being at the right place at the right time.

The North Carolina School of the Arts provided me with a direction to work in. It gave me the opportunity to hone in on my craft. We were acknowledged for our strengths and many times were cast against those strengths to stretch us in directions that, without this setting, we would either never get the chance to do or never seek out to do. This is one of the purposes of training in a safe environment where that penalty for error is minimized. Chance taking in learning skills is encouraged not hindered. An arts school allows those exercises that are meant to stretch artistic limits to occur. No one likes to fail in anything, though true failure is not my meaning here. It's more like falling forward. In taking artistic chances, most often I am leaning forward and thus progressing. Falling backward, or at least staying in the same space, usually intimates being more cautious and a bit on the safe side, doing the things that will not expand abilities. When skiing down a mountain, it is when you lean forward that momentum is gained and where there is the highest risk/reward ratio. The arts school is a place to expand. There are times when doing all the right things right, moving forward, and progressing do not translate to recognition. When that happens, it is important to evaluate. Were choices solid and bold or uncommitted and anemic? If the answer is on the solid side, then maybe it just wasn't time to be recognized, but it does not diminish the quality of work at any rate. Many times there are people watching when it is least expected, making it important to keep doing the best we can.

By living around other artists, their choices can be observed too, and it will inspire new approaches to work that may have never been considered. With all of the creative energy that surrounds a campus such as this, there is bound to be new awareness to a craft, how to approach it and how to practice it.

Having made it into the school alone provided an acknowledgement to our having some level of talent. We were now there to tune the instrument and learn to truly play it, to push beyond the safety of comfortable and play outside the lines. "Dare to be bad" was a phrase exhorted in this process. This was the perfect setting for that, to find out where the balance was of giving too much or too little, by going beyond our comfort zone and exploring different intensities and methods, having it preferable to go overboard and able to pull it back than to not give enough and have to manufacture something not true to raise the level up. But in order to do so, you have to let loose and not hold back. How to do that was part of the instruction we were receiving.

In my case, I usually worked very hard at not letting go so much, trying not to look bad, to appear always in control in performance, almost as if trying to be the director watching from the outside while playing the character. This held me back from really finding out how far I could go in playing the character and discovering it to be one of the things I needed to learn, to trust the director and to fully commit myself to the character. This is a step every actor must take. I did learn. It is something to be constantly aware of, continually making a conscious effort to let go, to make choices that may be wrong for the part, but allowing those choices help shape the right ones for the part. It is a bit of trial and error. The school environment allows this type of exploration which is not always available in the professional world.

As an example of what I am talking about, look to actors like Tom Hanks, Jack Nicholson, Jim Carrey, Robert Redford, Robin Williams, Tim Roth, William Macy, Meryl Streep, or Sir Anthony Hopkins to name a very few. These actors stretch themselves and almost always find a way to create unexpected choices, consistently giving unique and fascinating performances. There are many more, of course; but with this limited list, you can immediately think of a few roles that stand out without much thought.

As I said earlier, we were here to tune our instrument. A program of dance classes in jazz, tap, and ballet no less rigorous than what the dance majors took (just fewer), voice lessons as intense as voice major classes, and other disciplines revolving around the arts to broaden our perspective and understanding quickly became our routine. Many classmates had backgrounds in something other than theater, so it increased the level of expertise in those classes dramatically by what they brought to it. We learned stage combat, gymnastics, juggling, tai chi, and yoga. All were very physical classes, yet one of the most physical of them all happened to be mime. Each mime class would start with stretching for up to a half hour doing exercises that were physically demanding, concentrating on strength, balance, and agility. Most classes lasted two to three hours at a time.

UNCSA is built on a hill with many stairs adding to everyone's overall conditioning. We walked or ran the steps. This sounds a little out of place saying something like this, but this happened to be part of our overall physical development instigating strength and stamina, as we exercised everything, mind and body and, yes, spirit.

During this time, writing music, poetry, and lyrics started to develop. Peeking into my notebooks from that era, you would see that doodling also seemed important. Exploring all avenues of expression bubbled forth in this time.

Within the mime classes, we learned mask work, commedia dell'arte, character creation and development, and, certainly, classic mime technique.

Our class uniforms were leotards and tights. We all wore them. In mime class, we had a black hood that we would wear as well. Since most of what we studied required much exercise and physical conditioning, we were required to wear these every day. A few reasons for this were that it allowed us the freedom to move as dancers need to move, it allowed for corrections in posture or positioning in almost all of the classes, and it took us down to a base level of not relying on street clothing to influence character development. We could always add a hat or scarf or jacket to color the character we were working on. The women would also have a long black shirt that they would wear for the times that required the semblance of a dress. The skirts could also be used as capes. It is the intention to start with a minimal pallet and add as is necessary.

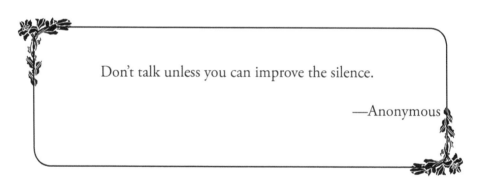

Don't talk unless you can improve the silence.

—Anonymous

CHAPTER
4

ASPECTS OF MIME

Mask Class

For our mask classes, we sculpted fantastic faces in clay and used paper-mache to construct them, finishing them off with acrylic paint. We explored using different body positions to express different emotions or attitudes and in wearing only our uniform and the black solid hood focused strictly on gesture and attitude. The hoods were made of a light stretch material and did not have eyes or mouth or anything cut out, but the material allowed us to see through the hoods enough to get around. Since mime was predicated on movement and expressing without the use of sound or voice, the language was portrayed by only body positioning. Wearing our hood created an expressionless face, so the body became the expression and not a grand or small facial movement. At this point, masks would be introduced into the exercise. With a fixed expression on each mask, it becomes the body's duty to give life and different emotions to the mask. The mask can then take on many more meanings than the one that it was designed for. A different actor will, many times, discover a new emotion by what he or she brings to it by way of body language. A whole new world seemed to open up to me, and I gravitated to it, completely intrigued and fascinated by it.

Classic Mime

Nonverbal communication preceded speech. Before formal language, stories were told by movement and mimicry. When words were finally developed, no one told the Italians, so they kept talking with their hands. That is where the saying "When in Rome, do as the Romans do" comes from. Otherwise, it would be "When in Rome, say as the Romans say." But that is not how the saying goes. That is why they finally developed the commedia dell'arte in the 1500s. I just made that up. Actually, the Italians did create the commedia dell'arte, or the art of comedy, which is a form of theater and entertainment that incorporates stock characters with certain personality traits portrayed predominantly by costume, masks, and gestures. Traveling their shows from town to town, the actors encountered different dialects and could not always communicate in the presiding language. The action and stories were told with gestures and circumstances that the audiences would recognize. As this theatrical genre became more popular, the crowds would be in tune with who was whom by what they wore and how they acted leading to using the same characters in different situations yet the characters staying true to their personas.

Even today we still see the influences of commedia in our theater, television, and movie industries. My purpose here though is to give you a little background to the development of the mime artist of today.

The modern-day mime is actually descended from the ancient Greek playwrights such as Plato, Sophocles, and Euripides:

Required Ability

Pantomimes cannot all be artists; there are plenty of ignorant performers who bungle their work terribly. Some cannot adapt themselves to their work; they are literally "out of tune"; rhythm says one thing, their feet another. Others are free from this fault but jumble up their chronology. Still, it seems to me that we have no right to visit the sins of the artist upon the art: let us recognize him for the blunderer that he is, and do justice to the accuracy and skill of competent performers.

The fact is, the pantomime must be completely armed at every point. His work must be one harmonious whole, perfect in balance and proportion, self-consistent, proof against the most minute criticism; there must be no flaws, everything must be of the best: brilliant conception, profound learning, above all, human sympathy. When every one of the spectators identifies himself with the scene enacted, when each sees in the pantomime as in a mirror, the reflection of his own conduct and feelings, then, and not till then, is his success complete.

But in pantomime, as in rhetoric, there can be (to use a popular phrase) too much of a good thing; a man may exceed the proper bounds of imitation; what should be great may become monstrous, softness exaggerated into effeminacy, and the courage of a man into the ferocity of a beast. (Lucian, Of Pantomime, second century AD)

The amphitheaters of the time were large and seated thousands of people. Acoustics and amplification were limited to the power of the actor's voice. Not everyone heard the dialog further back in the arena. They sat and had to rely on the gestures to supplement their understanding of the action of the play. Facial expression was equally important to identify emotions. It is here that a base makeup and a highlighting of the eyes and mouth came into favor.

Because of the language barriers and difficult travel conditions, entertainment was very much restricted to being performed locally by nearby artisans. That is the importance of the creation of the commedia dell'arte.

But as you can see, the mime or pantomime stood and stands as a separate entity. Dance and acting intersect yet remain their own art form requiring different skill sets. Dance is more of a celebration, not requiring one to know any specifics, but is more aligned with feelings and essences. Meaning and understanding can be left with more leeway to interpretation than to hard and fast communications, much like music. Acting demands a heavy balance of the verbal sound and, even when heard in different languages, can evoke meaning by aural rhythms, inflections, intonations, patterns, pauses, and intensities. Take this away from the actor, and there is a definite loss of comprehension. A mime though must deal in comprehensibility, a consciousness with intention. If he fails to be understood, the illusion is shattered, and confusion sets in the minds of the audience. The mime must balance between dancer and actor, yet project the art's own silent expression.

A few of the well-known characters are recognized in play characters and in entertainers' personas. Harlequin is seen in the character of Harpo Marx, for example. Harlequin, or Arlecchino as he was originally known, is predominantly a dim-witted fool with flashes of brilliance. He is a mischief maker always hatching schemes that typically fail. Columbine is his love interest, but that does not keep him from chasing the other ladies. He moves with great agility in spite of his stupidity and ignorance. Even today you will know him by his costume of brightly colored diamonds. Harlequin is one of the most recognized and popular characters to come out of the commedia dell'arte.

Columbine, the sharp and witty servant who loves Harlequin, always tries to improve Harlequin's status. Maria from *Twelfth Night* is likened to her. Dainty and demure on one hand and then audacious and ill-mannered on the other, depending on the play, she almost always plays on the lusty romantic side with Harlequin being the object of her affections.

The Doctor, a pompous old man, quite taken by himself speaks with great authority about things he knows absolutely nothing about. Known for his half mask covering his nose and forehead, his character would be well versed in the seven deadly sins. All of his life's learning comes with complete lack of understanding of any of it. Most often he comes off as crazy, forgetful, and without morals. Pantalone, also an old man, is his friend who is more action than words. Both are stingy types—the Doctor because he does not have money and Pantalone because he does.

Pantalone is usually the financial force in town. Wielding power or any other usable resource, with a very tight grip, he also is a terrible letch always on the make of the pretty women who cross his path, which is why he gets along so well with the Doctor. Pantalone normally the oldest of the old, having money or not, lives the life of a miser. His mask shows massive wrinkles and an overly abundant nose.

Capitano, the bold loudmouthed braggart, always boasts of his great conquests. *Cyrano De Bergerac* provides a good example of this character. Being devious and greedy, it is not unusual for it to be found out that he does not even rightfully hold that title. By his swagger and bluster, he often covers up his true cowardice. Typically dressed in full military regalia, the Captain looks the part, but his true colors most often shine though in the end.

Pierrot, one of the most popular of the players, is the character associated with the biggest influence of the white-faced mime of today. Known for his oversized white clothing with large pompom buttons and a clown ruff collar and some kind of skullcap or hat for his costume, he plays a dreamy, romantic, heartsick figure. Though additionally known for his innocence now, before the eighteenth century, he was more of a prankster who also verbally abused the other characters.

Scaramouche is in the same vein as the Captain but not quite as large. He is an arrogant and sarcastic fellow.

Scapino manages to muddle up everything and thus needs to flee the situation. Scapino's name means "escape." And even if this means running from his own devices, you will find him plotting in his villainous way throughout the action.

I have only touched a little on these characters. Each known by different names at times, their characteristics help to identify them to the audiences, whether the dialect or language is understood by them or not. They encompass much more specific traits in their personalities and attributes than I am going into here, but I hope you get a feel for a bit of this theatrical history, the Italian commedia dell'arte being the most famous of the historical lineage to mime.

The Japanese have the Noh theater which uses many mime elements. American Indian cultures use pantomime in their rituals. There are examples of historical significance to the origins of mime from early Chinese eras to South American civilizations. So across the world, these traditions have made their way through time and cultures influencing communication, ceremony, and rites without the dependence on language.

It would be too simplistic to say pantomime is from one thing. It has come to be by fusing storytelling, dance, gymnastics, martial arts, gestures, and emotions and generally presented without the benefit of verbal language. Music and props are often added for effect. There is no one great definition for this art since it evolved from bringing many art forms together. And now its impact has inspired dance, clowning, magic, and other performing arts.

Mime itself is not a simple art form, and I do not wish to give you any idea that it is. There are movements that can be learned rather easily, yet that alone will not make someone a mime. It is with the movement that I must start. It will be to that foundation I apply thoughts and stories.

Isolations

I start with isolations, moving one part of the body at a time without moving the other parts, starting with the head, back, forward, and side to side. Then, trying to imagine that my head is on a platter and with the same front to back or side to side, without the shoulders or body moving, I work at keeping the head level and not tilting and then moving to the shoulders and leaving my head and body in neutral. I push them forward, then back to neutral, back, then back to neutral, up, and down in the same way, both together, and, then one at a time, one back and one forward, reverse, and all without the chest moving so only the shoulders do the exercise. I repeat this over and over, loosening the muscles isolating the chest in the same manner keeping the lower part of the body and my head completely still. Arms and legs require a whole new set of exercises. My hands work extensively to create different shapes and objects. I work on grabbing and releasing, flattening and relaxing the hands, and incorporating finger exercises, thereby giving fluidity to movement. The entire body is worked this way, from contorting the face from big and wide open to closed and scrunched up, lifting the forehead up and keeping the rest of the face normal, and trying to move only one part of the face at a time to working my feet and ankles. The whole body is incorporated to bring the illusion of mime to life.

Mastering body movement is really only the first step in this process of becoming a mime. This is an ongoing process, discovering how my body moves and to what effect. Much is learned by working in front of a mirror. As with dance, body positions reflect certain attitudes and meanings. Use of space and knowing my relationship to it is critical.

The Wall

For example, in creating a wall (one of the popular moves), that wall must occupy space. When creating anything invisible, there must be an adherence to the actual physical properties of the objects and things being created. Only after those elements are established and solidly so can I manipulate the object and do something different with it. A wall is immovable, and that must be established. It has density and shape and weight. With my hands, arms, and body, I must be true to those characteristics in order for the illusion of a wall to be read by the people watching. Certain movements must be exaggerated to make up for the object's invisibility. In actuality, when I put my hands on a wall, there is merely a touch. There is no illusion to the actual wall. It is hard and takes up space. There is no need to exaggerate any movement. But with the object not there, it is necessary to augment a movement to give it those characteristics.

And once it is created, the laws of physics still apply to it. If I have established the wall to be in a certain spot on stage, I must be totally aware of where that spot is when returning to it. Otherwise, the illusion is ruined. In the same way, if I take a glass out of a cabinet on an empty stage or empty space, I must remember that the glass stays constant in size with a specific weight when I handle it. It must stay uniform throughout the movement. If I put it down on a countertop, I must be true to the dimensions of the countertop and the placement of the glass on the countertop. If I walk away from both the glass and the countertop, I must be accurate in returning to the same precise spot; and if I want to return the glass to the original cabinet, I must be sure of where I placed the cabinet. I have not mentioned here going to the refrigerator and getting the milk, pouring the milk, drinking the milk, returning the milk to the carton where it came from, washing the glass in the sink, where the sink is located, drying the glass, and putting it back where I first took it from. All of the objects must be first created here and established as real in the minds of the audience. This little exercise shows the need to understand space relationship and my body. I must create an entire environment with very specific movements and gestures.

That is the physical side of mime. When layering that with emotions and feelings, a new world is embarked upon. Imagine the cabinet placed above adding anxiety to getting the glass and maybe on top of that discovering the milk is sour, for example. Then add to that the water from the sink being scalding hot. What types of reactions do these inspire? It is said that acting is reacting. The reaction to the stimulus is of utmost importance. These are only a few ideas on how to make a simple act of getting a drink from the refrigerator more interesting to the viewer. These were the kinds of exercises that I would go through.

As I say, once the illusion is set and adhered to, it could be modified. The wall could start pushing back and a ceiling could start to lower, but the characteristics must stay the same. Only now the conditions of the objects add a new wrinkle to the presentation.

When a storyline and imagination are added to everything mentioned above, movement and illusionary mime takes on a much more complete and complex experience. And to be really good in putting it all together, there needs to be a training that encompasses a wide spectrum of subjects.

The same holds true for any artist. To reach the soul of the art, there must be a depth of understanding with an awareness of the world in general and in areas more specific depending on your focus and thrust. This takes study, reading, experience, and practice. And there can be no cheating, for that will be exposed in the performance or the art.

Finding My Center

"When the dream is big enough, the facts don't count."

The point of self-evaluation started somewhere around nineteen years old or so. I can't say reevaluation here because I cannot remember ever doing the initial evaluation. The world looked upon me with a very critical eye, or so I concluded. In a competitive society, aren't there a multitude of people, it seems, whose sole purpose is to keep us from outperforming the next guy? Instead, I looked at the people who encouraged me along the way and looked to my own victories, no matter how great or small, as the stepping stones that got me to this point in time, looking to what I already had achieved. By focusing on the accomplishments, I built a protective wall to stand up to the barrage of "No," "Not this time," "Sorry, you won't do," "Thank you. Next," and "No, no, no" that I encountered at every turn while working on making an impact. There had to be that place where I could go, deep inside of myself, cutting through that negativity, finding the reserve within myself to repel these criticisms, these rejections. Also relying on family and friends as advocates to help mitigate and deflect the rejections, no matter how great or small (because even chipping away can cause major wounds), thus any temporary setback did not grow to a major defeat with possible lasting results.

We were all given the ability to imagine and to dream. If imagination and dreaming were not exercised, they would recede from lack of use. These are tools that not only artists use and practice. Many business leaders mark off days and weeks out of every year specifically to think and ponder and dream and imagine. As an example, think of the contributions of Walt Disney, Steve Jobs of Apple, Thomas Edison, Henry Ford, or Donald Trump. All had or have extraordinary imaginations and vision. They implemented actions to those thoughts and found a way to go beyond conventional wisdom to create empires honoring their dreams, backing it up with hard work and diligence based on continual dreaming and envisioning. It takes practice.

A great pianist can miss a week of practice and the audience may not know or miss a day or two and the teacher may not know, but the pianist will know even with only one missed day. It is the same for any artist. The integrity of the art and artist is one of the underlying motivation's main pillars. The dreams and visions inspiring hard work and discipline, truth and honesty, creativity and inspiration, and fear and acceptance are other artistic virtues; and there are more. There are a multitude of reasons and combination of reasons people pursue their art. Some are driven to it, and others are driven away. Some cannot live without it, and some die because of it.

Infatuation for something pushes us to begin many things. When the infatuation fades away, hopefully a core of love and passion will keep the pursuit of achievement an ongoing motivator. For so many of us, life takes us down roads we would never have imagined and redirects our progress with pragmatism winning the day. Art takes on new ways of expression, the road less traveled, maybe not as we imagined it. It was this way when I started college, with starts and stops and ups and downs trying to figure out where I would make a mark in the world, knowing it not to be assembling sandwiches in a sub shop. A passion in me was reignited learning to be an actor, building skills that allowed me to become a mime–actor as well. Passion can be rekindled if the spark and desire are nurtured. Returning to college and going to UNC School of the Arts felt like this to me.

The curriculum incorporated mime, as a wheel on the training vehicle, not the entire vehicle. Also within the School of Drama, classes in phonetics, voice and speech, script analysis, period and style, dialects, stage combat, fencing, singing, jazz, tap and ballet, period dance, yoga, tai chi, body relaxation techniques incorporating different massage forms, and performance projects were required. We studied and performed Shakespeare, Moliere, Congreve, Chekhov, Strindberg, Ibsen, Shaw, O'Neill, and many more playwrights. We took classes outside of our main curriculum in lighting and sound, set design, and construction to give an overall understanding to the different components that go into all of theater production.

We all rehearsed every evening from after dinner to 10:00 or 11:00 p.m. After that we would go back and learn our lines and do required reading or homework for the next day. There was very little downtime, but we had fun because we were doing and creating and growing. Not everyone worked on the same project or play at the same time, so we always had the anticipation of someone else's performance. There were recitals, concerts, and dance performances to attend and always something fascinating to do or see.

Intensive Arts

In addition to the three trimesters of this training, each year between Thanksgiving and Christmas break, we formed our own groups to produce a performance of our own writing and creating. It is called intensive arts. We worked long hours for about ten days, and then the last few days before break, we would watch performances from morning until night. Like anything, there were outstanding concepts done well, and there were some that did not hit the mark. It was more about the process than the end result. It was here that we could absolutely "dare to be bad," of course wanting to be good as the result. We took chances and reached outside of our comfort zones. One year, I took part in a group project producing a practice-intensive cabaret show. Another year, we created a biographical documentary research project on Henrik Ibsen. Undertakings on two complete ends of the spectrum, but interesting just the same, they both concluded with a performance. The straps of the regular routine were off so we all could let loose and brainstorm without faculty involvement. It really wasn't much different, but it felt different.

This provided us an opportunity to create something from nothing. So when later on I had the chance to write my own show, I called upon those experiences as a template.

As an older student, living on campus felt somewhat restrictive, and I found an opportunity to move into a house off campus. One of the piano professors at UNCSA, Bruce Moss, and I became good friends, so renting a room in his house helped him defray his overhead and got me off campus within walking distance of the school. We had many great conversations. Two Steinway grand pianos took up a third of the living room. He taught private lessons to a few students on them. He'd play often, preferring one particular piano that he had picked out himself. The other grand piano was passed on to him as an inheritance gift from his teacher. Hearing Bruce play confirmed my choice of going into a different direction than piano. He is superb. We drank a lot of coffee then, and sometimes when I smell coffee brewing, it transports me back in time to those days and house. After two years, I moved out because he had fallen in love and would soon be married. They needed the room. I found another apartment to share.

The Farmyard and Indulgences

The winter trimester of my junior year at UNCSA had me cast, along with classmates Rick Gardner, Monica Gross, and Ellen McQueen, in two four-actor shows. One was a new play. It was *Indulgences in a Louisville Harem* written by John Orlock and directed by his friend, our teacher and mentor, Marty Rader. The other play, *The Farmyard*, was also directed by Marty.

Rick Gardner played the professor, and I played Winfield Davis in *Indulgences*. Playing this part demanded more of me than almost every other role thus far. It required me to speak my lines and the professor's lines in two completely different voices; and since this had to be timed to the professor's mouthing of the words, there had to be a consistent delivery of each sentence, thought, and idea. Here is an article from a Minneapolis production which opened the night after we opened in North Carolina:

> Indulgences in a Louisville Harem *is a very funny and very touching play. Set in a Victorian parlor in 1902 Louisville, it concerns two sisters well on their way to spinsterhood. An unsolicited package arrives at the door containing, among other things, "Mrs. Whiting's New Book of Eligible Gentlemen," a mail order catalogue of men. Naturally the two ladies order themselves a man, one Professor Amos Robillet, a mesmerist from the St. Louis Institute of Science and Populism.*
>
> *The professor soon arrives with a trusted colleague, Winfield Davis. It's here that Orlock springs his most audacious plot device. The professor is mute and, though he mouths his words, Davis speaks them for him. He speaks them in the professor's*

voice, mind you, and swears they're even the profes-
sor's ideas. He's merely the go between. To prove it,
he has the professor hypnotize him, even though he
has to speak the mesmeric mumbo-jumbo himself.
This is one of the funniest scenes I've ever witnessed.
Seeing Davis slumped down into a trance, even as
he says, "You're eyes are heavy, you're getting sleepy,
you're turning into a chicken," is a typically imagi-
native Orlock device. But far from letting it go as a
mere gag Orlock develops the notion into a character
study. Davis, we learn, was always tongue-tied until
he had to become the professor's mouthpiece. Then
brilliant phrases and ideas started tumbling out.
He's even able to propose marriage now, eloquently,
for both men.

The two, of course, are charlatans and the
ladies discover it but, just as dreams of the two will
be destroyed, the playwright gives them an out. They
can still marry the two, cads or no, and Orlock
makes the ladies decide. One does take off after these
jolly rogues, one stays back, content to live with
her dreams and wait. (Mike Steele, Drama Critic,
Minneapolis Tribune)

A letter turned up in a keepsake box of mine written by our
director and teacher Marty Rader to us, his cast, and in sharing a
part of it with you, it gives an idea of what goes through a director's
mind once the show is about to open. This reflects the type of guidance an actor gets when he or she is lucky enough to have a director
who is very clear with what he wants from the production. In spite
of this show's success, the buildup to it proved to be nerve-racking
and uneven. In what is known as the magic of theater, many shows
come together at the last moment. This happened to be one of those
productions. During the final dress rehearsal when things were pretty
tense, things had not gone smoothly. Marty could not be there the
evening of the opening night, for some now forgotten reason, so he

wrote us a letter including his notes. The notes won't mean much here because they were specific to the moment back then, but the general thrust of his concerns is embodied in the part I quote here. What is conveyed here is the director's love for the creation and the teacher's love for the process of a show, embodying the encouragement, frustration, personal understanding of each of the characters, and the hope of great performances:

Well—you say you have your best performances when I am not there to see—so prove it!

Energy! Pace! Pick up cues! Energy! Let's cut out this trust crap and beat the hell out of the script.

There is too much thinking and not enough believing. You're not doing—you're pretending to. That has got to stop.

There is not a single moment in the script that can't be played by any of you! There is not a single moment in the script where we should be aware of the actor preparing for his "moment" thinking about it—let these characters alone!!

They are not you! They do not want to be you. I don't want to see you. Let them alone to live their own lives. They want to be free so that they can laugh, enjoy, romanticize, dream, pretend, have memories—all unencumbered by your intellectual grasps.

Attack moments, beats—don't slide into them!! We, the audience need to know when things are happening.

Enjoy tonight—it ain't gonna be here again! Be magnificent. You all can. (Marty Rader, Director)

Like I had mentioned before, we pulled this one together to be a fine success, but it wasn't an easy go through the rehearsals. The words Marty wrote did make an impact and we did let go, and each performance got better for each of us. We were not perfect. This is a show we all wished we could have had the opportunity to perform for a much longer run. Three or four shows seemed too few. That's what makes live theater such a challenge. Going to an arts school allowed us to develop and stretch. This show and Marty's letter reflect the process each actor must go through to hone the craft. Marty did see the rest of the shows and joked that if he had known the letter would have made the huge difference it seemed to, he would have written it two weeks before to avoid the aggravation. But he knew we were learning, and this was how our learning curve evolved.

Immediately following *Indulgences,* the same four of us went directly into rehearsal for *The Farmyard. The Farmyard* was talked about for years after we graduated. I know this because of my visits to the campus years after. The new students would recognize my name because the legacy of the show had lived on. *The Farmyard* was remembered as a powerful theatrical event. It dealt with rape and abortion, two very sensitive subjects. The dialog contained simple and minimal lines. What moved this play so forcefully were the subjects and how the characters dealt with them. In the actor's exposition of the thought processes, there would be pauses lasting thirty to sixty seconds between lines. This is an eternity on stage if you haven't experienced it. The silence had to be filled with specific intentions so the audience could almost see precisely the mind at work augmented by the slightest and succinct gestures, where a thing like the movement of a finger, a tilt of the head, or the closing of an eye spoke volumes. This was a very low-key, tension-filled show that had a pulse, more like a throbbing. It pulled the audience in as if the whole theater breathed in unison. But what I remember most is the silence and occasional sob in that silence and then the almost collective sobbing once the play ended. We took our curtain call and left the stage as the audience sat for what seemed to be minutes before anyone moved to leave, many of them weeping visibly. This happened after each performance. Touching an audience in such a way really humbled us. Of all the shows I have performed, this one show taught me that the sound of appreciation can come in different forms.

Because none of us received large parts in the Shakespeare plays in the fall, the four of us were cast together for these two shows, while the others were cast in the major production on the main stage for the winter term. The winter semester was a highlight of my time in college. Of course, there was a bit of regret in not playing Shakespeare in all of us. That gave way to realizing we had the prime situation. Sometimes there are gems hiding in disappointment. Yes, these were gems.

The Prime Time Mime Company

In March of 1978, my classmate Jay Colclough and I auditioned for and got summer jobs working at Busch Gardens: The Old Country, in Williamsburg, Virginia. I vaguely recall the audition and tend to think it happened on campus.

After working the previous summers selling advertising; waiting tables; selling theater season subscriptions for McCarter Theatre in Princeton, New Jersey; teaching mime and acting; playing the piano in restaurants; and anything I could think of that would help me get through school, this job felt like a step forward in my career.

Going to Busch Gardens to work and the prospect of making money doing mime at a theme park turned out to be exciting and a huge stepping stone, and getting the gig instilled a nice boost of confidence for me. Throughout my time at UNCSA, many schoolmates from all disciplines got summer jobs at places like Carowinds, The Lost Colony, Six Flags, and a host of other theme parks and theaters in the south. The level of talent that is hired is tremendous. This would be a feather in my cap. Having Jay to work and share an apartment with provided a sense of security. Anticipation overrode any trepidation, and a looseness kept anxiety at bay.

The mime troupe brought together by Busch Gardens consisted of four. We came up with the name Prime Time Mime Company. Jay and I worked well together from our mutual training at UNCSA which was now quite extensive. Dominic and Laura had different strengths in their own right. Dominic was an experienced mime with a lot of street mime under his belt. Laura did not seem to be as experienced but had a very sweet disposition and worked hard learning new techniques. We worked for a week and put together skits and routines leading to six half-hour shows per day for six days a week for ten weeks. Unfortunately, Dominic did not make it past the second week. His street mime routines were a little too bawdy for the family-oriented audience. He had some funny material but lacked subtlety bordering on the uncouth. This turned out to be just the wrong venue for him. So we reworked our routines with Laura and moved forward.

In essence, we were street mimes with no formal stage for us to do an actual show, improvising much of the time weaving through the crowd, interacting with them with invisible walls, pulling ropes, and mimicking walks and attitudes to the delight of the onlookers. Standing motionless as mannequins for periods of time, the park guests were not sure what to make of us. This led to wonderful reactions from the passersby.

We wore no traditional whiteface makeup and used only eyeliner to accent our eyes. With the heat of the summer, we were always glistening, giving us a plastic look. That helped. Standing absolutely still and then making a sudden body shift in a robotic move would sometimes create a crowd, with the young ones asking each other if we were real or not. A brave young soul would gingerly approach to give us a touch to confirm we were fake when we would suddenly take a new position and let out a blood-curdling laugh, scaring the entire group like the start of a marathon race when the gun went off.

Not satisfied to staying in the same spots, we explored other entertaining possibilities and happened upon the fun house, each of us positioning ourselves at the beginning, middle, and near the end of it. Instead of just walking through and being merely amused, we startled the daylight out of them. Some of the reactions were priceless. To top it off, getting a paycheck for doing something that we got a kick out of doing made it all the better. Without a doubt, we had as much fun as the guests.

The Threepenny Opera

Starting my senior year in college could not have begun any better. Having found a new house to live in across town added a new element of growth. Over the summer, Bob Murray, our director, let me know, to give me a bit of extra time to prepare, that I got cast as MacHeath or "Mack the Knife" in *The Threepenny Opera* by Bertolt Brecht and Kurt Weill based on *The Beggar's Opera* by John Gay. If there had been any doubt about my capability of being an actor, my UNCSA career justified all my hopes and dreams. When presented with the lead, much rides on giving a solid performance. Heading a cast carries weight, with certain pressure, but this wasn't new to me so I welcomed it. The leads of the show were double cast for the show, meaning the parts were to be shared, as they do in a repertory company. Of course, it would have been great to have the role to myself, but I did see the value in this type of arrangement. It provided opportunities for more of us to shine.

Since moving to a new part of town, learning the lines and songs for *Threepenny* required time, which I had given while driving around Winston-Salem in my 1974 white Ford Pinto station wagon. I wore gray funeral gloves and black bowler hat, to help assume the character of MacHeath, keeping an eye out for back alleys and dark corners of the city, imagining this to be nineteenth-century London and scoped out potential hangouts for conducting nefarious business, and found this particularly effective in transporting me back in time to the rainy, moonless, dangerously dark, dank, and foggy London just before the 1838 coronation of Queen Victoria. Trying to capture the gritty, cold-blooded nature of this man, I would imagine killing unsuspecting patrons of the local late-night waffle house pretending it was a brothel. In 1838, London must have had waffle houses. Don't you think so?

Imagine, if you will, my "carriage" parked around the corner of the building, undetected by the local constables, allowing me to slip unnoticed into the waiting booth of this questionable establishment of decadent delights. The overworked madam of the house would saunter over to pour a lusciously hot cup of coffee, gently flipping the upside-down cup sitting on the table to its open-mouthed position with her long and graceful fingers (she must have done so thousands of times before) all the while looking deeply into my eyes finishing the pour and, before I knew it, thrusting her ample and sticky menu of delicacies into my waiting gloves.

"Would you like cream?" she cooed.

"No, just hot. The hotter, the better, and keep it coming," I responded slyly.

Then her hand, with no hesitation, plucked the bowler softly from my head and placed it quietly in the seat across from me.

She smiled as she said, "Good to see you, Mackie. What can I do for you? Do you see anything you'd like to wrap your lips around?"

Before I could answer, a bloke across the room distorted his face in a disapproving way toward me on his way out the door. I sipped my coffee once, retrieved my bowler, paid the lady, and disappeared out the door. Swiftly and quietly, I killed the man. No one looks at Mack the Knife that way and gets away with it. After dragging my first victim to the river, I returned to my coffee, ordered an omelet, and returned to modern-day Winston-Salem with no one the wiser to my actor's exercise.

I enjoyed the ludicrousness of it all and will tell you the different scenarios that I developed helped me build a rich and textured character. With only half the rehearsals, employing this technique provided the way to maximize the time I did have to create it.

In the professional world, there is always an understudy waiting in the wings or the coming and going of cast members throughout the run of a show. Having to work side by side in learning the part would prove to be a great experience. Bob Hoshour shared "Mack" with me. His performance was smooth and catlike, while mine gravitated toward the more rough and threatening. Both worked. Splitting parts also helped the faculty divide meatier parts for others in our class. It should be mentioned here that double casting also occurred for the spring repertory tour the seniors would be traveling in the following months. There were only fifteen of us, and this arrangement allowed for all of us to get the taste of performing under these conditions with some great roles.

When a show closes, it adds so much to whom you are, but there is also a sense that you left a part of you behind. I suppose in a bigger sense that can be said of many things that come to an end. When *Threepenny* closed, I felt exactly that way. It began to sink in that my college career had finally entered its last stretch. Yet, while my time at UNCSA had given me the opportunity to reach further than I dreamed possible, as the long awaited repertory tour arrived, my future hung out just around the corner.

The Spring Repertory Tour

The repertory tour became one of the tremendous opportunities availed to us at UNCSA, if we made it to this stage of our education as seniors. We prepared three shows for tour: *The Three Sisters* by Anton Chekhov directed by Tunc Yalman; *Under Milk Wood* by Dylan Thomas directed by James Dodding, a guest director from the Rose Bruford College in England; and *Patches*, a mime show written by us and directed by James Donlon.

Along with the actors, the tour included seniors from the tech department, who designed and built the sets, all the lighting and sound, and all of the logistics in transporting them in two 26-foot trucks. This was no small production to travel, unload, set up, wire, run the show, break it down again, and pack it for the next performance. Now also take into consideration there were three separate sets with different requirements for each performance. Each actor, alongside the techs, participated in all the phases of this grueling routine.

For *The Three Sisters*, I played Kulygin, the cuckolded teacher, this being one of the few parts not double cast. Most of the other parts were, giving everyone an opportunity to play a bigger role. This did mean many more run-throughs for the benefit of the actors to freshen up before a performance.

Under Milk Wood did not need to be cast in this way. Due to the nature of the play, we all played multiple small parts with the action guided by two narrators instead of the one as written for the radio performance. We adapted it for a life on the stage.

Patches materialized from our mime classes, and completely original written by our class, this presentation followed the previous year's same concept for its senior class repertory tour. The prior class received rave reviews for their work, and ours would continue in that vein with a very entertaining show as well. *Patches* provided a showcase for each of us to take the spotlight. This contrasted so from the other shows. Performing it gave us a very unique feeling, possibly since we conceived it. This experience proved to be the seedling that germinated and would sprout later when I had the opportunity to create my own show.

Remember the mask class we participated in? In an extension of that class, we created what we termed the functional object masks by building masks with everyday items to create silly and funny effects. Two of my fabrications made it to the show. One I named the Jersey Juicer.

This mask's construction started with using a beer ball keg. If you haven't seen one, it's a plastic ball holding about five gallons of beer! Naturally, it had to be emptied prior to its second life as a mask. What we do for our art, eh? I held onto one for a while hoping it would come in handy for something. This made sense because it seemed unique. Being made of a thick plastic made the ball some-what easy to work with. I carved out a place to put my head into. On top I carved out a small circle and inserted a funnel-shaped bowl large enough to hold a few pieces of fruit, removing the bottom of the bowl to be able to add inner workings, but not big enough to let the fruit fall through. For the mouth I just cut out a smile and later glued a piece of thin, see-though black cloth to the inside of the ball allowing me to see out though nothing could be seen from the out-side in and then fashioned the nose out of an outdoor faucet fastened through another hole. For the eyes, two holes were cut allowing the insertions of two 5-ounce juice glasses, painting the beer ball orange while using black paint to outline the mouth and the edges of the juice glasses, to highlight the eyes and eyebrows. I then stretched thick elastic straps on the back to hold it on my head, pushing the back of it into an arrangement of wire clothes hangers, wrapped and taped in a type of catcher's mask configuration. Inside a container was attached that could be removed and filled to be then connected with tubing to the inside of the faucet.

In performance, wearing the mask I made my appearance on stage juggling the fruit, usually just oranges, then caught one in the funnel top and added the next two pieces of fruit, then pulled out a potato masher, and reached up making it appear I was crushing the oranges. Actually, it originally had been designed to be a crank that attached to the side of the mask, but I never found the right part. Pulling one of the juice glasses from its socket, I proceeded to hold the glass under my nose and open the faucet to fill the glass with juice from the hidden container inside the mask. To add a twist, instead, it changed to green Gatorade juice which always seemed to get a laugh. Gross things make people laugh I determined.

This became part of my solo show. I would leave the filled glass sitting on my antique trunk positioned off to one side of the stage and out of the way for upcoming pieces and then exit. The filled glass would sit there through a couple more skits appearing later to discover it. I would pick it up, look at it quizzically, and then drink the juice. Instead of getting a laugh, for some reason this always elicited a response from the audience of *Ewww!* which gave me the greatest kick. Gross things make people laugh and go *Ewww!* I determined, amending my prior determination.

My other functional object mask, as we called them, was constructed in the shape of a piano, fabricated out of quarter-inch plywood and black cloth. The ears were made of cardboard and black duct tape. The eyes were made of brass finger cymbals and the eyebrows made with brass tacks, woven with brass wire. For the nose, I used a trombone marching lyre. The keyboard represented the mouth and made to fit a melodica, a mini piano played by blowing into the end and pressing the keys sounding like the crossing of a harmonica and an accordion. It took a while to figure out how to make it stay on my head, but I finally came up with the idea to use a construction hard hat, bolting the visor of the hat to the back of the mask. Except for the mask being too heavy, this would have done the job. To keep the mask from tipping into my chest, a series of bungee cords to act as chin straps and head straps crisscrossed around my head, with draping black cloth over the back. To make the instrument work, I discovered it necessary to create a mouthpiece using a tube to reach my mouth.

Naming him after different piano manufacturers, I called him "Lowery Kimball Steinbald." When performing with this mask, wearing all black with a long black tuxedo tailed jacket, making his way to the center of the stage, standing at attention, perusing the audience, giving a slight bow of acknowledgement, he would produce a page of music or a cutout eighth note and attach it to the noseclip lyre. Reading the music, he then played one note by touching the keys of his "mouth" resulting in "Lowery" being a bit taken aback by his own sound. As the piece progressed, "Lowery" became more confident and ended by playing a version of "The William Tell Overture" commonly known as the theme from the television show *The Lone Ranger* from the 1950s and 1960s.

Sadly, both of those masks along with my other original masks and equipment were stolen out of my car a couple of years later. Although I fabricated and replaced much of what was taken, those two presented more of a challenge finding the right materials to recreate them. They took up a lot of space when traveling, and I thought it best to keep them as a great memory, although with the possibility always to bring them back lurked in the back of my mind. They just never got done. I still miss those guys. They were silly, unique, and fun. Who knows? Maybe I can bring them back someday.

> *…an inspired short piece with a little piano used as a mask and character. The brief piano piece is superbly zany, as the piano-headed, tails-clad figure stands on the stage for a concert, placing his music on his clip nose and more or less rocking the ivories that are his teeth. (Oh, yes, and the piano has eyes and ears, too.) (Genie Carr, The Sentinel, Winston-Salem, North Carolina, March 4, 1979)*

> *In a very funny sketch, for instance, a student stands with his head encased in a toy piano whose keyboard forms a toothy grin. (Jim Shertzer, Winston-Salem Journal, March 4, 1979)*

Our class toured the three shows from North Carolina to Connecticut for about six weeks. Along with our class were the members of the tech crew. We would travel with a couple of large 26-foot trucks loaded with our sets, equipment, and costumes. Upon arrival to a destination, everyone was required to help with the setup of the stage. We would do a sound and light check and if time allowed a run-through. Some of our stops on the tour required only one or two of the shows to be performed, while others would have all three, a different one each night. Immediately after the show, we got out of costume and makeup and took down the set and put it back on the truck.

This occurred at the time of the Three Mile Island nuclear plant meltdown. We happened to be performing on one of our stops not too far away from it in the Amish Country of Pennsylvania. So while sane people were trying to get away from it, I invited friends and family into the area to see the shows. There doesn't seem to be any lasting effects of all of that, so far.

Bill Cole introduced himself to me as a Latin teacher at a private all-girls school, the Madeira School, in McLean, Virginia, when we met while he visited Busch Gardens the summer before. Through him, I was able to book all three plays at his school and, because of Bill's insistence some time later, came up with my own solo mime show.

The tour culminated my college career, the culmination of the tour being a showcase in New York City attended by a large contingent of agents and managers. Also in the showcase were other acting schools, such as Julliard, Yale, Carnegie Mellon, and New York University. This was a big thing for us. Out of this showcase performance, we all hoped to catch the eye of the agents and managers in New York. Doors opened because of them. Without one the road was much tougher.

As it turned out, we generated a lot of interest across the board. I had a few interviews as did most of my class. Some had more than others, but we were all thrilled. Michael Thomas represented me as my agent. He represented many big name talents, but the one that always got a lot of attention was Margaret Hamilton, who played "The Wicked Witch of the West" in *The Wizard of Oz*.

Graduation from UNCSA followed only weeks after ending our tour. We were all now anxious to get on with our careers and hope for the best.

On June 2, 1979, I received my Bachelor of Fine Arts in Drama from the University of North Carolina School of the Arts, having just turned twenty-six and ready to move on to the next stage (pun intended) of my life. Going on for my master's degree? Forget about it! It's out of the question! It's not that I wouldn't have enjoyed the journey a little more, but life beckoned.

All the world's a stage,
And all the men and women merely players:
They have their exits and their entrances;
And one man in his time plays many parts,
his acts being seven ages.

—William Shakespeare

CHAPTER

5

New York City and Beyond

New York City, New York

The way I calculate it, this started the third act of my life—the first being my childhood, the second being my high school and college years, and now entering into my career.

The first thing that needed to be done was to get my head shots and resume together. Michael Thomas recommended me to a New York photographer, Larry Lapidus, who took some terrific shots. You can never be thankful enough to find a talented photographer. In an industry that tosses out pictures on a glance, I know his at least opened a few doors for me. Pounding the pavement is part of the game. I stood in many long lines for an audition. Without the help of Michael Thomas, who sent me on many more auditions, it would not have been possible for me to get them otherwise. An agent is crucial in this business. They work hard over many years to establish trust with industry professionals who are in need of the right person to fill their cast or project. Michael sent me out for commercials, soap operas, and television shows. At the same time auditions came for Broadway and off-Broadway plays.

That summer, a Polaroid camera commercial came my way. James Garner and Mariette Hartley were the spokespersons for Polaroid but were holding out for a bigger contract, so the advertising agency Doyle, Dane and Bernbach created a backup campaign. I shot for one day, costumed in a British Royal Guardsman uniform, while the little girl took pictures of the guards trying to get us to smile. The commercial never aired because Polaroid paid Garner and Hartley what they wanted. Bummer!

In August I landed a part in an off-Broadway musical called *The Ragged-Trousered Philanthropists*. Although I did not get a lead part, the ensemble remained onstage much of the time.

The importance of having an agent or manager or both is to get through doors to be seen. This is only part of the equation. Also important is to be a member of the Screen Actors Guild (SAG) if you are doing movies or film, Actors' Equity Association if you are doing theater, or the American Federation of Television and Radio Artists (AFTRA). They are the three unions that actors usually belong to. There is also a musicians union, but that is another area.

To get into any of the unions, there are requirements, other than the dues, that you must meet to be eligible to get your card. There are benefits to belonging to the unions if working in the profession is your ambition.

Doing only one more commercial or other film job would earn me an SAG card and present more opportunities.

Earning my Actors' Equity card could be done several different ways. I could get a job in an Equity show if the producers could not find anyone already an Equity member able to do the part to the satisfaction of the management. That is the most direct way.

By taking the off-Broadway show, the opportunity to attain membership came by way of touring for a two-week run satisfying the criteria for me getting an Actors' Equity card.

With an Actors' Equity card in hand, the auditions available to me would be multiplied greatly. Not having the card meant open calls where thousands show up for a very few parts. That translates to long lines, long days, and long odds in that scenario.

The membership also guaranteed a certain pay scale once I did get a part. As it was, I made about $100 a week for *The Ragged-Trousered Philanthropists*.

The musical took place at the Labor Theatre, whose name and politics meant nothing to me other than me getting a part in a show in New York City and a way to get my Actors' Equity card, hopefully leading me to more work. The book of the same name was, as I found out, the virtual guide to the Socialist Labor Movement in England from the turn of the century 1900s and afterward. I still didn't care. I needed the Equity card.

The show opened to positive reactions. We were not panned and had a nice little two-week run in New York leading up to the time of our tour of another two weeks traveling down to the George Meany Center in Silver Spring, Maryland. George Meany was the president of the AFL-CIO labor union for a period of time, and this was the center for teaching and implementing labor doctrine. I still didn't care! I needed the Actors' Equity card!

Once we were on the road and performing, everything seemed to be going very well. After five days of performing the show, we were told that the tour would be cut short to one week. This meant that I would not be getting my Actors' Equity card because the criteria would not have been met at this time.

Did I feel bamboozled? You bet I did! Here we were performing at a union mecca and we got screwed out of a week's work, a week's pay, and most importantly qualifying for my membership into the Actors' Equity Association. This unforeseen setback came after investing three months in a project that turned into nothing more than what was now considered to be a waste of time. Getting a nice New York credit on my resume, mixed with a very sour disappointment, only felt like a setback. It actually was a baby step forward in some ways.

Things were not that bleak at all, really. Auditions kept going, callbacks to soap opera readings provided hope, and I had taken a job in Red Bank, New Jersey, teaching mime at a dance studio to supplement my income.

Sometime near the end of November, the phone rang.

Bill Cole had an idea for me to consider.

Our species is the only creative species, and it has only one creative instrument, the individual mind and spirit of a man. Nothing was ever created by two men. There are no good collaborations, whether in music, in art, in poetry, in mathematics, in philosophy. Once the miracle of creation has taken place, the group can build and extend it, but the group never invents anything. The preciousness lies in the lonely mind of a man. (John Steinbeck)

The Call for a Mime Show

Bill Cole, if you recall, taught Latin at the Madeira School. Six months had now gone by since the School of the Arts Repertory Tour. Bill called to ask me to bring my mime show to Madeira and four other private prep schools in the area.

I told Bill, "I don't have a mime show."

He said, "Get one."

I said, "I don't have one."

He repeated, "Get one. I want you to put together a mime show, and I will put together a tour of five schools that you can perform at for $200 a night."

I asked, "When do you want it?"

He came back with "I'm looking at the second week in February."

"That sounds great, but I still don't have a mime show."

"Then get one. You can do it. I'll set it up down here," he said one more time.

And then I told him the thing that would lead me onto a road I would never have guessed.

I said, "I will get one. I will put together a mime show."

Just like that, an opportunity that I had never contemplated before now started with an idea and a faith in me that I did not see coming.

This seedling began to sprout and grow into what would be my eventual mime career.

How fortunate to be teaching mime in a studio. Creating a show from scratch presented many problems. Having a space to work from took care of a big one. I started by making a list of pieces already developed from my years in class, estimating how much time it would take to perform each one, and then setting out to build upon unexplored ideas creating more skits. This process continued even once the show had enough material, my never being afraid to try a new piece out on an audience, rehearsing it first and then placing it into the show somewhere anticipating its impact on the flow of the show. In the beginning, though, most of the pieces were new; so its trial by fire, shoot from the hip, wild wild west approach had a certain high-wire act feel to it. No nets!

93

What do I recall most about that time? By far, it had to be the constant contemplation that went through my mind during my waking hours—from pulling ideas from the extremely simple, like hammering a nail into a board, and thinking hard how to make that into a funny bit, somehow, to reaching in for deeper, darker thoughts concerning suicide or the electric chair and how to discover some way of touching on things that are not easy to understand. I went to sleep thinking about it, woke up thinking about it, and spent most of my days formulating the show. The mask piece would account for about seven minutes, and my life cycle piece would be around nine minutes. Jersey Juicer and Lowery Kimball Steinbald would be another four minutes. After adding up the pieces already prepared, only creating another forty-five minutes to an hour more would be required. Over time some pieces got cut completely with new ones taking their place, while some just got tighter and did not need to be longer to carry its effect. Skits that worked very well in the beginning but somehow lost something or lost poignancy were modified or replaced altogether. Definitely a maturing process occurred demanding it necessary to produce stronger vignettes making each show better than the last one. This creative process never changed. If something did not work well, it would be rectified or dropped.

The first shows were done on a silent stage with whatever lights were in place. Props were set up on both sides of the stage, and I would move from skit to skit with only a lights out or lights up cue. This was not a technically sophisticated show. The thought process that guided me was to merely keep it simple in this regard. Time would almost always be an issue for setup and run-through. The best way of handling this would be just to have someone flip a switch on and off. I never knew what level of lighting engineer would be working the show, so taking this element down to the lowest common denominator took one element out of the stress mode.

For my initial tour, I performed two dress rehearsals at the studio with my students watching. Having a temperature of 102 didn't keep me from getting my first dress rehearsal in. Crunch time added some urgency, and needing this rehearsal I just went for it. Adrenaline carried me that day.

"The show must go on," as the saying goes.

I brought *Body, Mime, and Soul,* the name of my show, to life in February of 1980. For the next ten years, it took me down roads never imagined.

At the time I still went to auditions. With a show still very much in its infancy, there were no guarantees that this mime thing would mature into anything at that point. I auditioned for *Barnum,* a new musical on Broadway, got called back, and then did something unwise, changing my audition. This is something so risky since casting directors liked what they saw in the first audition. Because I changed the audition, I did not reinforce my initial audition. It is like they were looking at a different actor, so why chance it? In this way I feel that I blew a great opportunity. Oh, sure, there's always next time. As it turned out, next time never came. I started to get interest in my mime show from colleges and other places causing me to shift gears not even recognizing that happening until New York appeared in my rearview mirror, so to speak.

Who knows how this mime thing would turn out had it not been for a kick-start five-school tour? It would be safe to say, at that point anyway, I probably would not have come up with the idea of writing a show by myself. The lure of making a thousand dollars in one week motivated me.

While preparing my show, more information about how and where to book it came my way, finding that colleges and universities paid very well for this type of show. I knew a little about it from my time at UNCSA, but not a lot. Some basic research helped get names and contacts to possibly book a few more shows.

Each performance moved me up another rung on my climb. Positive feedback encouraged me from the beginning.

The Homecoming

Onstage, the hooded figure is trying on masks and with each change of false faces, his body acts differently. Now it moves jerkily, now slowly. In the audience, mostly high schoolers, there are occasional words of encouragement to the figure, occasional laughs, and occasional applause. The hooded figure says nothing.

Wearing a mask reflecting sheer disdain, he sits at the piano and begins to play "Do Nothing 'Til You Hear from Me." That could take a while.

Who is this masked man?

A little later, he will take off the hood and be revealed as Ken Alcorn, returning to Hightstown for a performance at Peddie School. He still won't say anything. His show "Body, Mime and Soul" is mime, and the signature song is a little joke.

The show meanders through some very human foibles. In some cases, what he's up to is apparent from the start of a skit, and in others the realization dawns gradually. In the latter cases, you can hear individual members of the audience "catching on," a few at a time. (Tom Blackburn, Sunday Times Magazine, May 4, 1980)

Growing Pains

The process of booking entertainment on a college campus would not be as easy as wished for. Most of the entertainment schedule is already set four to eight months in advance, more in some cases. For me to book anything for the finish of the 1980 school year would be difficult at best. Only asking a few hundred dollars per show helped generate business at this point, a small enough amount that some schools still had in their budgets. Making lots of phone calls generated some interest with actual bookings around the area. What were needed now were publicity materials: things like brochures, posters, pictures and biography, contracts, mailers, envelopes, stamps, pens, markers, and a fax machine. Back then fax machines were slow and long-distance phone calls costly.

Starting this journey on a shoestring budget, it became evident very quickly I needed money. If only plan "A" would suffice.

I will swerve away for a moment to share with you a bit of the survival part of being in show business by telling you about my job waiting tables at a very nice Hilton Hotel restaurant. Yes, this fits the stereotypical actor–waiter scenario. Although a hotel restaurant, there was nothing mediocre about it. We prepared Caesar salad tableside (something that would one day play a significant part in my life), as well as Steak Diane, Fettuccine Alfredo, cherries jubilee, and Bananas Foster. The scallops wrapped in bacon we served came on a long skewer set ablaze and gallantly paraded from the kitchen to the table, the flames extinguished by covering them with a waiting plate cover and plate on the food gurney pushed in behind us. We then prepared the entrée and served it. This display presented an impressive sight when we had a large party and more than a few flaming swords entered the dining room, adding to the fine dining experience augmented by a bit of showmanship.

A tall, thin, older headwaiter named Ralph taught me an immense amount about fine dining service. I remember him being a very proper and well-educated man with an air of haughtiness about him. One bit of advice I still share is to save the money from the great nights; and if you are going to blow any money, blow the money from the meager nights, instead of the other way around. It was good advice, and I thank him for that. It is so funny how we pick something up and it lasts a lifetime. I paid a little tribute to him by fashioning one of my paper-mache masks after him. Inspiration comes from the strangest places.

That experience would prove to be very helpful in the years to come. There were times when I needed to supplement my career with an infusion of cash, and waiting tables could fit nicely into the schedule.

While performing at a few colleges that spring, I learned about the National Entertainment and Campus Activities Association (NECAA), later changed to the National Association for Campus Activities (NACA). It is an organization where student activities directors and their students on the school's activities committees would have the opportunity to come to a conference or convention to meet and then book the entertainment they would have on their campuses. The agents representing the artists, lecturers, bands, novelty acts, or, in some cases, the acts themselves would come set up a booth or two in an exhibit hall to book their acts. There were regional conferences in the fall and some in the spring and a national convention in the winter. Acts would submit materials for review to be chosen for a twenty-minute showcase which were scheduled throughout the event. Getting in front of the audience who actually booked the shows provided the best exposure. By the way, all of this costs money.

After joining and then signing up for a booth in the exhibit hall for the Southeast Regional, that year held in Savannah, Georgia, I designed some marketing tools to decorate my booth and hand out to prospects.

My cousin Rich Grote, also a freelance commercial artist, and my brother helped me produce my first brochure. We did a photo shoot. Rich and I spent a lot of time in his dark room developing the pictures. I will always be grateful for their time and talent. Doing graphics now on a computer can accomplish in an hour what it took a week to do in those days! But we accomplished the project. Once, for my poster picture, I pressed my made-up whiteface with my open hand next to it onto a copy machine, adding the graphics, and voila! A mime poster! It got me through that first season until I could afford to do it on a more professional-looking level.

Not until the following year would any semblance of a tour coalesce. Chances to perform came irregularly in the beginning. Yet, the responses and feedback from my performances only encouraged me to keep going. With each show, tangible progress created lots of energy and momentum. Newspapers were interviewing me giving encouraging press. Going into New York and performing on the corner of Central Park South on 59th Street and 5th Avenue across from the Plaza Hotel doing my street mime routines, I passed the hat to earn a few dollars. This kept me on my toes. New Yorkers are almost always rushing to the next place to wait. In order to capture attention, I stood as a statue. It's prevalent everywhere nowadays, back then not so much. In the hustle-bustle of the city, that stillness made impact. Once there were a few people watching, I broke into my act.

The time came in September for the NECAA Southeast Conference. I had booked my room at the DeSoto Best Western ready to go. Having never been to Savannah, I showed up a little early to see a little of it. Getting to a destination early eased my mind. It's a habit I learned in theater, because in theater, being late for the curtain will cost you your job. Besides that, now as a professional, I had a reputation to build.

Upon checking into the hotel, posted on the bulletin board was the schedule of events indicating the NECAA dinner would be at 6:00 p.m. Great! I had enough time to shower and dress. Dressed in jacket and tie, I innocently sauntered in, so excited to be there. It must have been very evident. After a few introductions, I soon discovered this to be the leadership dinner and not for the associate members, like me. One of the leadership members invited me to stay. It wouldn't be a big problem in any way. This very kind gesture helped me learn how the organization worked and who guided it. Consequently, they now knew me too. The story spread around the exhibit hall about the mime who crashed the leadership dinner. The best publicity I could have ever asked for came from my party crashing. It turned out to be a successful conference with my meeting many people that I would subsequently contact, leading to many eventual bookings.

The Northeast Conference followed the Savannah conference a week later held at Grossinger's Resort in the Catskills, famous for its entertainment affectionately called *The Borscht Belt*. All the great comedians from the 1930s, 1940s, 1950s, and 1960s, particularly the Jewish comedians, would go there for steady bookings. Tearing it down in the late 1980s made me a little sad because of its wonderful glimpse into an era gone by. Over the years the styles changed. The resort built on a hillside of the Catskills, with an almost labyrinth maze of hallways to get lost in, would invariably lead to a dining area or bar lounge. Many of us explored those with great gusto. But new replaces old, and time marches.

Having crashed one leadership dinner was enough for me. They would just have to get by without me. With all of these new contacts, my purpose to establish my show shifted into gear.

Attending these two conferences became a yearly tradition. Over those years I did get showcases at both of them, also earning the honor of being chosen to perform at one of the national conventions, that year held in a cold and snowy Baltimore.

The Little Rascals on television might be lost in today's world. Most people might know the names of Spanky, Alfalfa, Darla, and Buckwheat. I had the pleasure of meeting and getting to know George "Spanky" McFarland through the conferences we participated in. Spanky (I called him George), now in his fifties, traveled on the lecture circuit at colleges, corporate events, and celebrity golf tournaments talking about his days in television. His granddaughter booked his engagements. Not much about George had changed in his later years since being 'Spanky" in charge of "Our Gang." Not very tall and still stocky, he still had a wonderful presence about him. Jovial and gentle at every turn, we three had dinner together numerous times at the meetings. He loved talking about his golf game. He died at an early age of sixty-four in 1993.

Meeting people who were famous or were about to become famous was part of the joy of spending a few days at the conferences. One of my favorite stories came about because I had a bit of inside information picked up along the way that seemed to have no real import at the time and never thinking there would be an opportunity to use it. The Amazing Kreskin, a very popular mentalist, became a household name in the 1970s after many appearances on *The Tonight Show Starring Johnny Carson*. He had now taken his show around the country as I now did. As it turns out, he lived around the block from one of my cousins who always saw him walking his dog around the neighborhood. My cousin, years earlier, had mentioned this to me, and for some reason I remembered this little fact. As I mentioned, meeting fellow performers at the conferences always proved fun. At one of the showcases of a conference, I found myself standing next to The Amazing Kreskin and, recognizing him, turned and introduced myself, extending my hand. In shaking his hand I feigned a slight shiver at his touch, closed my eyes, and said to him as if seeing a vision, "Why do I see you walking a dog, on Atlantic Avenue in Point Pleasant, New Jersey? Does this make any sense to you?"

As I opened my eyes and looked him in the eyes through his black rimmed glasses, he had this very quizzical look on his face as I then smiled and again introduced myself to him. I snagged him at his own game! It caught him a little by surprise. We had a nice chat after that. Divulging my source would have taken away the fun. He chuckled once he knew I had gotten him. Magicians and mentalists never let on to their secrets, and that satisfaction would not be his either.

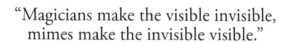

"Magicians make the visible invisible,
mimes make the invisible visible."

—Marcel Marceau

In 1980, there were already a number of mimes and mime companies on the college circuit doing what I intended to do. Trent Arterberry, a renowned and tremendous talent, inspired me greatly. At the time, he lived in New England and now is in Vancouver, still performing and entertaining. Tim Settimi, out of Atlanta, is a superb performer, blending his musicianship, juggling, roller-skating, clowning, and mime into a wonderful theatrical experience. Keith Berger, an extremely gifted mime, has gone on to form a physical theater company. The Quiet Riot mime team with Bill Mettler and Kevin

O'Connor from Philadelphia still perform. Joe McCord from the west coast and Shields and Yarnell known for their television show are also part of the scene. They too are exceptional. These were a few of many that I could mention that already established themselves as I got into the mix. My job would be to take a piece of the pie believing that a good show by any one of us led to more bookings for all of us, widening the market base.

As I developed my college presence, I also had the honor of being elected and serving a two-year term on the Associate Member Advisory Board of the National Association for Campus Activities. Now a mime finally got to speak at the table of ideas, yet grateful that others now viewed me seriously as an artist among my performing peers and a leader representing them in a significant position.

More than that, NACA honored me by nominating me for Entertainer of the Year one time. I must have been doing something right.

An actor dreads the recurring dream of not knowing his lines. Mine? Thinking that staying in one place long enough, discovery as a charlatan would be inevitable. The fear of being branded as a fake, phony, or pretender haunted me. Maybe it's what drove me to give it my best shot at becoming a household name the hard way. Fear of failure can be quite motivating. The other side of that is the fear of success. The question for that is: "What do you do if you do become famous? Will you be able to continue being creative and live up to the expectations?" That thought rumbled around from time to time, but I rejected that anxiety simply by looking at how many times I kept meeting each challenge that came along. To counter the chips, digs, and rejections one receives along the way, the successes, big or small, remedy and diminish the discouraging moments.

Do you ever notice that in times of pain and suffering and mental anguish, the clock seems to slow to almost a standstill, while the times of joy and happiness increase the speed of time and before you know it, it is over? In truth, the clock is the constant, and we are the variables. It sure would have been nice to have road signs on this journey. Maybe there were some, and I missed them.

> The men who try to do something and fail are infinitely better than those who try to do nothing and succeed. (Lloyd Jones)

As stated earlier, looking back and seeing the turning points is much clearer than when the choices are in front of you, which brings to mind the poem by Robert Frost (1874–1963):

The Road Not Taken

Two roads diverged in a yellow wood,
And sorry I could not travel both
And be one traveler, long I stood
And looked down one as far as I could
To where it bent in the undergrowth;
Then took the other, as just as fair,
And having perhaps the better claim,
Because it was grassy and wanted wear;
Though as for that the passing there
Had worn them really about the same,

And both that morning equally lay
In leaves no step had trodden black.
Oh, I kept the first for another day!
Yet knowing how way leads on to way,
I doubted if I should ever come back.
I shall be telling this with a sigh
Somewhere ages and ages hence:
Two roads diverged in a wood, and I—
I took the one less traveled by,
And that has made all the difference.

And so life goes for us and has gone for me. All that had gone before led me to this new journey.

An actor takes the sting of rejection on a continual and unrelenting basis. We do what we do because it is who we are. In this process of "dancing on the skinny branches," as I call it, the risk of the fall is as great as the thrill of the flight. Anyone who auditions for a living knows that a thick skin is needed to protect the wound that a simple little "no" inflicts. As a pen knife is to a large tree, doing little damage nick by nick, over time they can cut deeply the pulp. So too the simple innocuous "no" can do also to your soul. It is with the occasional triumph that a period of healing occurs and protects from further damage, at least for a while.

Transferring my energy to producing a mime show seemed like "dancing on the skinny branches." *The Road Less Taken* now very much offered the fork in the road and a definite one indeed. New York had not beaten me. Not enough time or failures occurred for me to consider that. The opportunity to climb another ladder of success emerged, figuring that when I made it to the top level, all that would be needed was a jump of the scaffolding to get me to where I wanted to go as an actor. However this worked out, I committed myself to doing my best and keep trying.

"No" wasn't going to stop me. Determined as I could have ever been, for some reason, putting together a show to tour seemed to energize me. Maybe it gave the feeling of having a say in my own destiny and not relying on someone else to approve me for a role. I believe it to be more than a maybe.

If something else came up that would lead to success, it's all the better. I would be no worse off and have a viable product to sell and perform as well.

We are the music makers,
And we are the dreamers of dreams,
Wandering by lone sea-breakers
And sitting by desolate streams;—
World-losers and world-forsakers,
On whom the pale moon gleams:
Yet we are the movers and shakers
Of the world for ever, it seems.

—Arthur O'Shaughnessy

CHAPTER
6

PRIME TIME MIME

The Prep School Tour

This is in answer to the question that has now been asked to me for over thirty-five years now: "When did you first become a mime?"

The answer is 1978, when I worked at Busch Gardens and got my first professional mime job as a member of The Prime Time Mime Company followed by teaching mime and then creating my solo mime show *Body, Mime, and Soul* for tour one cold week in February. It is the name also chosen for this book. Having by that time taken mime classes for over five years, this art form provided me with a powerful artistic weapon in my arsenal along with acting, singing, dancing, and piano playing. Trained, prepared, and ready for my opportunity to take this career to the next level, how could I not take the challenge of traveling a show? Whether reaching success or suffering failure, responsibility for either result would be mine with no one else to blame. The road that offered a choice of paths would not run the parallel course once anticipated. It took me, again, to new destinations.

The "what ifs" of a life are fruitless because it is impossible to speculate accurately. The saying that "Life is not a dress rehearsal" is true. My father told me to do the best with the information that is available. If more information is needed, fine, but do the best with what is there and make the decision. And then he would quote one of the great baseball players in history, Satchel Paige, "Don't look back. Something might be gaining on you!"

Bill Cole had done what he had promised by lining up five prep school performances contained within the one week. They were all within a short driving distance of each other, and it could not have been a better planned tour. It is the formula that I tried to pattern my future tours around. So many variables within each new booking exposed the wants from the needs for a quality performance.

Coordinating those needs for the performance spaces took some planning and forethought. I had to figure out what would be optimum in different places provided. A theater was always the prime venue, yet not every stop provided me with one making it necessary to make do with six or more 4 × 8 risers. It was necessary for an offstage area for props and a place to catch my breath. Certain items requested that I didn't carry myself like a chair and a music stand were required. Getting a piano, let alone getting a piano in tune with all the keys working properly, came through most of the time but always had me crossing my fingers.

No two shows were identical. By never being on the same stage for even two nights in a row, there was no way that one formula would suffice. The only continuity and constant was that it was me, my ideas, and an audience. Tweaking the order of the show until finding how best to swing from one particular skit to another turned out to be an art form unto itself. All this sculpting was crafted to carry the audience through a wave of emotions, fast, slow, upbeat, sad, funny, and tragic, weaving a tapestry of an experience. Most of the time, modifications and adjustments were needed because of the space or technical considerations. It guaranteed that the show always remained fresh and like a new experience.

It would have been nice to have some of the workload split up. Having a partner, a manager, or a techie to travel with crossed my mind from time to time. The truth is that giving up control in any manner of something I built from the ground up felt wrong. Possibly, this could be seen as shortsighted and maybe so. In some ways I often felt like a Don Quixote never finding my Sancho, a trusted fellow adventurer. Standing on the stage performing alone, writing music or poetry and lyrics, or developing skits alone grew out of a need to be responsible and, it might be added, a need to feed my ego as well as my stomach. If it failed, the finger had to be pointed at me. If it succeeded, a part of me could enjoy that immensely, justifying another day to tilt at windmills by my lonesome and maybe briefly get the feeling of conquering them. It is something that took only a little time to get used to, because I found I liked the bit of solitude that came along with it.

The February tour gave me so much insight to what needed to be done. The shows were well received with each lasting about two hours. In the beginning, each piece needed extra polish, also realizing that some pieces would work some nights but not others. Being consistent was important, but not all situations of performance were the same with care given to modify and flow to what the conditions provided. With no time to get hung up on what I did not have, making the show succeed in any condition came as part of the territory. There were shows without stages, on the floor without the benefit of even a riser, performed in entry halls of student unions and lobbies; on platforms in cafeterias, libraries, museums, and living rooms; outside at the bottom of the hill with students sitting on the hill; in lecture halls, gymnasiums, bars with dance floors, bar stages with dance poles, and ballrooms; in the morning, afternoon, or evening, midnight shows, lights, no lights, large venues, small venues, with piano, civic centers, convention halls, with no piano, prisons, chapels, churches, classrooms, art studios, convalescent homes, assisted living homes, psychiatric wards, and television studios; and on the college green and Rathskellars. These places were the canvas where I painted the magic of mime. A theater was where I designed my show to be performed. The theater was the place that best suited my concept and performance to be seen. No matter where the stage would be set up, though, I tried to make it as much of a theater experience as possible. The set skits were used to ground the presentation. Improvisational skits grew out of the spur of the moment and expanded that way by need.

To give an element of surprise, I coaxed unsuspecting audience members up to the stage, putting them in unusual situations to play off of their reactions. Adding the audience participation in this way brought another dimension to the performance giving each performance a personal touch and uniqueness. No two people react exactly alike, so it is important to always be aware. From the audience's perspective, they usually found it to be always a relief not to be picked on and tantalizingly fun to laugh at a friend or someone they knew getting the "volunteer" treatment. Picking someone out of the audience can be tricky. Many times I would try to find someone extremely reluctant to come up to the stage. If the person next to them or nearby was overly thrilled at the prospect of seeing their neighbor put on the spot, I would immediately turn and "volunteer them," letting the shy one off the hook and putting the mocker on the spot. It worked more times than not. Already a bit flustered at the spotlight, they usually were terrific foils to my tomfoolery.

A simple gesture or look from them at the right time could lead to a theme that I could use throughout the entire performance. Comedy loves repetition well placed. The time at Busch Gardens, the street mime, and improvisational classes helped me hone those skills.

Ken Alcorn, a professional mime from the Mercer County area, portrayed the foibles of human nature using only steps, gestures, movements, and physiognomy in an extraordinary experience in the art of mime in the Rathskellar.

Anyone stopping at the door to investigate the entertainment for the evening must have felt a bizarre tingle seeing the "Rat" in an unusual character—the "Rat" was silent. The audience was totally absorbed in Alcorn's recreation of our daily lives.

Their expectations were continuously changing and growing with his control of the stage. He had a tremendous rapport with each of them, and when he challenged several people to participate in a scene, they were apprehensive but eager to experience this type of performance. (Maria DeAngelis, The Signal, Trenton State College)

There were standard requests to help generate interest in the show on campus by doing a ten-minute to half-hour teaser around the campus and teach a mime workshop to the drama students. This involved doing some street mime around the campus, usually in high-traffic areas like the cafeteria at lunchtime. If we had flyers to hand out, I did that too, followed by teaching a class. After the class, usually it would be time for me to set up the show and have a run-through with lights and sound if available. I needed this time to stretch and practice. Performing on either a full or empty stomach played havoc on my energy levels, so eating a light snack or sandwich about three hours before the show satisfied me. The few hours before the show were used for whatever needed to be done for the perfor-mance that night. At the one-hour mark, I started warming up and going over the backstage area checking that props and everything were in place. At half hour before curtain, I painted my face and got into costume. Showtime! Some schools wanted a question and answer period after the show, which I happily would provide.

Attending conventions, making phone calls, booking the show, touring the show, setting it up, breaking it down, packing it up, unpacking it again, repacking it and driving it, setting up travel arrangements, making props, and rehearsing were all part of my job description, as well as sewing costumes and banners, designing a set that folded into a suitcase, and fitting into a couple of trunks that would pack to fit under the bed I made for the back of my Volkswagen bus. And to keep money flowing, I waited tables, sold advertising and theater tickets, played the piano, bartended, worked for a moving company, painted houses, worked construction from time to time, and put my hat out while doing street mime in New York, Baltimore, Washington, D.C., and New Orleans (I also worked at the 1984 World's Fair there too). I performed at birthday parties, gas station openings, cocktail parties, conventions and festivals, and even swimming pool parties.

Bars would host talent contests to lure in customers. I'd enter them to try to win the cash or prize, and I once won ten cases of Budweiser and fifty dollars in Dothan, Alabama, for a second place finish against a local dance team of about eight members. They split their first place prize so many ways with each ending up with twelve dollars and a little more than a case of beer. Times like that made me thankful for being a solo performer. The sight of ten cases of beer stacked up in my garage didn't last long. I gave much of it away to friends and had a party or two.

The Road

Once, when traveling back home to Dothan from Tallahassee, a blurb on the radio announced a stand-up comedy contest in Bainbridge, Georgia, a little town in lower Southwest Georgia, was scheduled that night; so continuing on home and retrieving my mime gear, I jumped back into the car and headed the seventy-five miles or so back down the road, performed, and walked away with the trophy and $100 from the preliminary round with the finals in two weeks' time. Although the prize for that would be inviting, after evaluating the crowd, I thought it best to stay away, after ticking off the local contestants who were trying to win. They made it known that returning to try for the grand prize ought to be closely considered. And of course, wearing tights and whiteface in a southern bar was risky anyway.

Just one more episode in survival on the road to the big time!

The toughest challenge to overcome was the lack of energy level of very small audiences. That would happen once in a great while. Having nobody show for a class happened every now and then. On a campus, students were not always free at that time. Once, when only two people showed up for a show, booked right in the middle of the final exam week, we agreed it would be silly to go on. Even though I always took the agreed upon pay, I left that night deflated. Fortunately, that only happened once.

The opposite feeling occurred when fifty thousand people watched the night I opened for Crystal Gayle at the Chattanooga Riverbend Festival. What a thrill! There were a lot of ups and downs from town to town. One of my bookings had me slated to open for a local rock band at a university in New York state in Geneseo, New

York, to the most hostile place I ever performed. The crowd building to a frenzy and cranking up for the band, anticipating the high-energy act that they were gearing up for, was puzzled over this sole figure on stage wearing masks and moving around silently. *Oh, what have I gotten into?* I thought with this great sinking feeling knotted in my gut. At the time, I carried a Polaroid instant camera in my trunk on stage for use in another part of my show. Grabbing it, I took a picture of the crowd. The flash caused many to appear to have red glowing eyes, while their hand gestures could possibly be interpreted as telling me I was number one. Upon closer inspection of the photo, they were all waving the wrong finger to come to that conclusion honestly. It is a picture of pure evil to remember that show by. The activities committee wanted about twenty minutes for the warm-up act. I only made it to ten when things started being thrown onto the stage. I thought it best to just get out of there, get paid, and move on. Recently, Martin Short's autobiography describes a similar-type show he had to deal with. He didn't return the next night for another opener. They hadn't booked me for a second night opener, or truly I would have done the same as Mr. Short.

Traveling a show from town to town, college to college, and stage to stage thrilled me. Each time I headed out for a tour, some lasting three days, some three weeks or more, it came with a sense of privilege to perform and pleasure to garner a paycheck at each performance, the reward of all the hard work. Sure, the money paid the bills, but it also validated my path.

Loading the van and heading down the road, my cassette tape was cued to Willie Nelson's "On the Road Again," the anthem for so many of us who were carving out a life on the road. Even now hearing it takes me directly to that era.

Aside from the paycheck, the joy of performing, and the life on the road, reviews like this added further confirmation:

> *He engages audiences by conjuring up images*
> *and characters in empty space. Though nothing is*
> *actually there, nevertheless they still see something.*
> *It is neither a hocus-pocus set of tricks, nor sleight of*

hand. It is Ken Alcorn's mime, and above all, it is entertaining.

Ken Alcorn can convey more in a set of gestures and physical movements than most can communicate in a multitude of words. Perhaps he is most articulate when he is performing as a mime—acting out plots, ideas and emotions without the use of words. Yet, he, like many mimes, does not receive a great deal of public attention for his work. Thus, he must set aside his muted stage persona and speak out for himself and others of this usually silent community. (Erin Campbell, The Student Magazine, Wake Forest University 1981)

Part of the joy and allure of showing up on a campus for a show came from being treated so specially by the student activities departments, students, and directors. My requirements for a booking did not demand many extras. A hotel room and maybe a meal or two covered most of my contract rider demands. Once on campus, my hosts would parade me around introducing me to so many people who looked upon me with a kind of wonder or total indifference. I certainly wasn't given quite the rock star treatment, but it often made me feel quite like a celebrity, enough to whet my appetite for a little more fame than I actually ever achieved. The people at many of the places I performed really did treat me as something and someone very special. Staying humble through all of this never really became an issue, because only a day or two later I would be brought down to Earth and back to making ends meet in the not so glamorous world of the day-to-day job. Many things kept it all in perspective. I drove all of those miles, filled the gas tank, stayed at motels in the middle of nowhere, and ate alone. Being alone through all of this allowed a lot of time to think, practice, and plan.

Poetry and the Piano

Road trips provided stretches of time to write lyrics to songs of mine to pass the time. Driving without the radio on gave me the solitude and quiet time to explore writing as one more slice of right-side thinking for me. Because of the need to envision the destination and the roads that lead there, it is said that this is a function of the right side of the brain thinking. The right half is the side that deals with space relations, abstract thought, and things that are generally not so much straight line or mathematical-type patterns. With that mode of thinking already switched on, writing helped pass large chunks of time on the long empty stretches of highway.

Creativity and expression take many forms in an artist's life. Playing the piano allowed me to have an outlet for the emotions that were difficult to verbalize. Music soothes the savage beast, as the saying goes. It didn't reach that level of ferocity, but playing let me pour those emotions into my musical interpretations. By this time in my life, I had already written a few songs with many more through the years. Writing poetry and short essays started shortly after high school. Once at UNCSA, I began writing more, and it probably had something to do with the one English composition class needed to fulfill the academic portion of my schedule. Writing gave me a level of confidence. In my own voice with my own words, my thoughts could be expressed. Back and forth to college and later, the tour required long stretches of driving and more frequently as time went on. Being on the road for weeks at a time, covering up to five thousand miles was not unusual.

The sanctity of my car gave me the quiet I desired to dream up and create new ideas for my show. It was there, while driving, that a melody would pop through for a start of a song that could later be expanded upon, along with the poetry and lyrics, ideas, and musings. Back then, cell phones did not exist, so that did not distract either. Driving the usually barren highways with only the truckers at night, for the most part, made it difficult to write in the dark, so I used a portable tape recorder for any thought that I felt might have merit. Typically, thoughts and ideas were preserved using a pad and pencil to scribble down the verses. Transferring the hen scratch to a legible document, scribble would be a kind way of saying it. But it worked for me. Later, driving gave me time to write the lyrics to songs I had written. Here's one of those that came from driving:

Trepidation
Ken Alcorn

When all the words I want to say
Decide to take a holiday
And leave us sitting silent and alone,
Every minute that keeps passing by
I search for just the lullaby,
A simple song to ease your cares away.
You never asked, I never said,
What's the cause of all this dread?
A kiss is all I really have in mind.
My heart is really beating fast.
It seems the moment's here at last.
I haven't felt this way since who knows when.
I didn't think I'd love again,
Or didn't know the how or when.
But then you came and brightened up the room.
The shadows seemed to disappear,
As you descended down the stair.
You smiled and instantly I knew.
Yet words still fail me this is true.
A silly kiss, I hope you'll see,
Will uncork the bottled words in me!

The 1980 Lake Placid Winter Olympics

Once committed to traveling down a road, the things that are on the other road are not as much of a concern. They can't be anymore. The new direction occupies the mind now. In my experiences,

I have found the great excitement of embarking on new journeys is most often at the expense of giving up the comfort of the known for the possible discomfort of the unknown. Relationships work that way. Sometimes when sharing a journey, a fork in the road is approached. The road or relationship may have had rough spots in it, and going down the new path is a good thing. And sometimes the reverse is true. The scenarios are all individual to the circumstances. Hopefully, when we look back at those times, we can say it was for the best.

Ready or not, the wind will be at your back, or you are facing a headwind. Crosswinds can blow you over without much warning too. You will find days with no resistance and possibly no assistance either. Dreams, aims, and goals are so important. How do you know you are advancing toward something without some destination in mind or when you are going to get there? Putting a date and time on a wish makes it a goal. Reaching that goal may not happen, but with a deadline there is a better chance that you will be significantly further along in the process than had you not imposed an ending point.

Finishing college, by its very nature, sent me onto new horizons. People I lived, cried, laughed, and worked with would take off, as I would, on courses never to cross paths with each other again. And so it is with many parts of our lives. That's the hardest part. We take a bit of them with us through life; a passing thought of them acknowledges that.

When relationships end, they leave lasting impressions on the heart. Romantic love seemingly imprints the deepest because it exposes our deepest emotions which can cause a vulnerability and susceptibility to pain and heartache. But the ending could be in business, friendships, or even nonpersonal relationships such as when a project or dream ends. When more time, love, and energy are invested in something or someone, this seems to add the burden of demanding a successful outcome. When the outcome does not match expectations, upset in one or many of its forms can take hold. Thwarted intentions can cause the same. Action does not guarantee success. Something practiced does not guarantee a product of perfection. It is properly practicing the right things the right way that will lead to desired results, most of the time. Remember there are no guarantees in this life. External influences can interfere and foul up every worthy effort. Yet, sometimes external influences add to the value. Taking pride in my work and giving my best, I found, left me with the fewest regrets about any particular outcome. I wish it could be said there were never any regrets. Even doing one's best doesn't produce desired results all of the time.

At this point in my life, a four-year relationship had just ended, and a new one emerged. The new road since graduation had changed the course of everything. Emotions also pulled or pushed me, playing a large part of the equation, as they always will. Distance had taken its toll and carried not a huge surprise. I had worked too hard to give up or even delay my career any longer. Choosing to move forward, not back, I now focused on creating avenues for my mime show.

The Winter Olympics had started and were in full swing in Lake Placid, New York. Excitement couldn't be higher for the US hockey team, with mounting tension for the possibility of a United States versus the Soviet Union face-off in the semifinal round of the hockey tournament. Speed skater Eric Heiden dramatically on track to break every speed skating record by going for an unprecedented five gold medals added great anticipation.

My then girlfriend, Barb, and I (yes, we were Barbie and Ken) had just finished watching the US team beat West Germany to advance into the semifinal round making the dream matchup a reality. On this wintery Tuesday night, minutes after the game, the phone rang. A friend of hers from college, now in New York City, had four tickets to Friday night's semifinal game. It happened to be the USA vs. USSR match. He offered them to her along with four tickets for what would be Eric Heiden's fourth race. He could not make it up to Lake Placid for the weekend and asked if she would be interested in taking them—no charge!

With joyful surprise, we nodded to each other as she answered with "Absolutely!" He would arrange to get the tickets to us the next day. Astonishment describes our state of mind just then. What a fantastic opportunity!

Having just come off my successful and empowering five-school inaugural tour, I needed only to arrange for someone to teach my mime class which was done by calling a classmate from UNCSA, George Altman, who lived in New York and kindly agreed to cover two of my mime classes. The director of the studio was none too pleased that this had been done without her permission even though the students would be in very capable hands with George. She was just mad I didn't get her permission first, which I concede was a valid point.

While waiting around for information about the tickets and their arrival, phone calls were being made, and we were getting anxious. By Wednesday afternoon we found out that the tickets would have to be picked up in New York. So we left for the city early Thursday, picked them up, and drove toward Lake Placid. We decided to take a room a bit further out for fear of not being able to find one closer in, driving to a little place just off the highway near Albany, New York. Memorably decorated in the 1950s, it appeared nothing had been upgraded since. Some would call it quaint, tacky but quaint.

We inspected the package of tickets and noticed a parking pass for the town of Lake Placid, the Olympic Village itself. We could drive our car directly into the town and park. Had this not been the case, we would have to park about thirteen miles away at the parking center called Marcy and then be bussed to town. That was avoided by this pass to our good fortune.

Friday morning came, and we headed to Lake Placid, driving to the freshly snow-fallen Olympic Village. The village buzzed with excitement. Colors of the Olympic teams danced around the mounds of plowed snow like the flashes of a Lightning Ridge opal. What a sight! There were no problems in getting past the checkpoint. Not surprisingly, it proved easy with the pass attached to the windshield. We found our way through the center of town and located a choice spot to park.

Walking around in this winter wonderland in the early afternoon of the hockey game, Lake Placid pulsated with excitement and electric anticipation. People everywhere with great smiles on their faces greeted each other as they passed. I felt a welcoming sweetness to this place that is very difficult to describe. A phenomenon that gripped the entire village was pin trading. Pins were attached to hats and jackets and would be swapped, bought, and sold. Pins from all over the world, from major sponsors of the Olympics, from towns, cities, and states, with certain ones catching the luck of having a great value assigned to them, gave people a chance to walk around with their hats on their hand ready to make a trade. They called this "The Pinner's Palm." You could see the traders everywhere as they hunched over their pins showing their collections to each other in hopes of a new find. More rare ones or the certain ones that carried significance would generate a high trade or cash value. In the end, my collection turned out to be a cheerful keepsake. There might be some value to it. (But then again, I thought Beanie Babies would hold their value.)

When finding out we were to have four tickets to the two events, we tried calling friends that Tuesday night to join us on our adventure. None could peel away on such short notice, so we were left with two extra tickets. Getting them sold before an event as big as this didn't really cause concern except I had never done it before. Instead of waiting until closer to the start of the game, the extra tickets were burning a hole in my pocket, so I brought them out to sell about two hours before the game. They sold quickly for $400 for the pair. Thrilled with that price because it basically paid for travel and dinners, I only later realized tickets were going for three times that or more had I only held out. No matter, being a bonus from the start, I had no regrets.

We made our way to the Olympic field house and took our seats sitting behind the goal, Row P, sixteen rows up. Great seats! The chants had already begun. USA! USA! USA! Four thousand people were here to witness a game between the Soviets, who manned their team with the best professional hockey players from their country. They skirted the amateur rule by having them listed as members of their army team. Nonetheless, they were a dominating team and had beaten the USA Olympic team only weeks before in a tune-up game in Madison Square Garden by 10-3. The Soviets had won every gold medal since 1960. In those Olympics, Herb Brooks, the current 1980 team's coach, had been a member of the USA's last gold medal-winning hockey team. Going up against this Soviet juggernaut consisted of a USA team made up of the best college players that could be assembled. Our professional hockey players were not allowed to compete in the Olympics. Back then the rules dictated for amateur athletes.

This hockey game has come to be known as "The Miracle on Ice." It was a very tight game, one that saw a tying American goal with one second left in the first period, a 3 to 2 deficit entering the third period with a dramatic come-from-behind victory defeating the suddenly humbled Soviets by a score of 4-3. There was no shortage of euphoric exuberance in Lake Placid that night. In one of the greatest athletic events of the twentieth century, if not the greatest, the stars aligned to shine on a team of Davids slaying the mighty Goliaths.

The town village pulsated and bounced, all except the two busses, which held the dejected head-in-hand Soviets. We walked right past the loaded busses. I actually made eye contact with one of them as he turned away to hang his head. The anguished disbelief they portrayed on their sadly pained and startled faces caused me to empathize with them, but only for about two seconds!

Barb and I ended up at a restaurant where we met Hans from Sweden. The entire town partied, and in this restaurant it seemed to be led by Hans wearing a very impressive mid-calf-length fox coat. As we learned, he shot each one of the foxes, or so he said, from his bathroom window back in Sweden. I had no reason to doubt him. He had lost his matching hat the night before at the Hilton Hotel. In full-celebration mode, he insisted we join him in going to a party in the ballroom at the Hilton. So we did. No sooner than we passed through the doorway of the ballroom, the band stopped playing and yelled into the microphone, "*Hans, we found your hat!*" as the lead singer waved it in the air. I knew then we were with some unique company. The band came over and returned the hat to Hans. In the course of the conversation, I shared that I toured a solo mime show. A member of the band asked me if I wanted to perform on their next break when they found out some of my equipment, costume, and makeup were sitting in the back of my car, conveniently parked in the Olympic Village.

Getting to the car a half a block away to retrieve my stuff happened in the blink of an eye. With no formal dressing room, the hotel bathroom suited me to apply the whiteface makeup and costume up. At the break, the band introduced me. My show lasted for about fifteen minutes, doing my mask piece, life cycle, and one or two short skits. The room quieted down significantly as I entertained; and considering the magnitude of the night in this little hamlet on such a raucous night, I felt that alone to be an accomplishment.

This is only another example of always being ready to perform at the drop of the hat, because it's never known when a magical moment will present itself.

While removing my stage makeup back in the men's room, a man from Norway handed me a Norwegian ski team pin in gratitude for my performance. He said a few very nice things and wanted me to remember my performance with his token gesture of giving me the pin.

Champagne kept flowing, and Hans kept ordering (and not the inexpensive stuff). Barb and I ended up staying at the house the band occupied in a spare room. The skating event scheduled early the next morning rolled around too soon for such a late night, and, unfortunately, we did not make it to see Eric Heiden win his fourth gold medal.

Later that day we said goodbye to Lake Placid and drove down to check into another room at another very quaint motel. Despite not having seats for the finals, we watched the USA beat Finland to win the gold medal, in another come-from-behind victory on a small TV set in the little motel breakfast restaurant overlooking Lake George with ten or so other patrons.

Anticlimactic on one hand but we still reveled in the euphoria of the time, and we somehow knew this event would be talked about for a long time to come.

Chattanooga Riverbend Festival

Another memorable event took place in Chattanooga, Tennessee. A couple of gentlemen who worked for different universities left their positions and headed up the Chattanooga Riverbend Festival. They hired me to do street mime at the festival but also to travel around the city to different places for an outreach program to bring part of the festival to those who could not get out. Performances by many of the booked entertainers, including me, were arranged for prisons, psychiatric wards, hospitals, and local businesses. This festival ran for ten days and attracted hundreds of thousands of people.

Of the many outreach performances, a half-hour show in a psychiatric hospital stood out, along with the performances in the women's prison. For those incarcerated, any type of outside influences seemed welcome to break up the tedium of the day. I know my audiences appeared grateful anyway.

In the psychiatric hospital, the office personnel escorted me to the room for the performance as the chairs were being arranged for the group about to come in. In the back of the room sat a tiny woman dressed in hospital-type clothing, scrubs or something on that order. She gently picked at her hair as if fluffing it, then pat it without really touching it, then picked at it, and then pat it again as if to make her presentable. Placing my show suitcase down in the front of the room was all that needed to be done to set up for the show. (For small performances I only needed the suitcase with a number of props and masks in it.) The choice of not putting on whiteface makeup knowing it could upset some of the patients came from past experiences with performances such as these. While waiting for the rest of the audience to show up, I turned and smiled to the woman in the back of the room, walking back toward her. She looked at me and smiled back, tilted her head, and rolled it around in a flirtatious way. Her eyes were heavily made up with heavy blue eye shadow and uneven eyeliner around her eyes. Her eyebrows were drawn on with thick, black, and crooked lines, red blush splotched on and not blended in on her cheeks, and her mouth surrounded by lipstick that looked to be applied while the stagecoach was tumbling down the side of the mountain.

I said to her, "Well, don't you look pretty!"

She blinked her eyes, tilted her head, and coquettishly answered with "Thank yewww!"

"Did you dress up for the show?" I asked.

"Oh yes, I did" she replied.

"Enjoy the show. Very nice to meet you," I said and then turned to get ready for the show.

On the cue from the coordinator, I took my position standing in the front of the room like a statue, perfectly still. The doors were opened, and my audience went to their seats. Remaining still as a statue until all were seated and once introduced, my body began to move in a robotic fashion and slowly transitioned to a live person and then started to pull the imaginary rope with it pulling me back until hitting the wall of what I established as an imaginary cube that surrounded me. Making my way out of the imaginary box by way of the imaginary door, I then pushed the box, and the box pushed back. I found my way back through the imaginary door which closed behind me. Noticing a small finger-sized hole in the imaginary wall, facing the audience my fingers stretched the small hole into one big enough to stick my head through at which time the larger imaginary hole retracted appearing to trap me. A few sporadic giggles broke the mostly silent room, when from the very back of the room, the tiny woman from earlier spoke in a very loud and sweet southern accent, saying, "If we did that, they'd put us in the little rooooommm!"

Should I feel pity or anything else at that instant? Knowing it to be a psychiatric hospital, the possible truth to her plaintive outburst took me a little by surprise. Would a momentary pause mask my racing mind? Have you ever tried to withhold laughter? If that ever happens, gently biting the inside of your cheek or your tongue usually does the trick to stop the urge. With this show only two minutes old and twenty-eight minutes to go, finishing it the way I normally would hit a huge brick wall. The best solution, to my mind, would be to break the silent mime character explaining all actions to help them recognize my intended illusions. Describing and introducing each new concept worked well.

This one show influenced me to always give assiduous consideration to my audience and be thankful that they never put me "in the little rooooommm!"

A few years later, for the 1985 Chattanooga Riverbend Festival, in addition to the rest of my scheduling at the festival, they contracted me to open for Crystal Gayle, one of the headline acts of the festival. The deck of a massive barge moored to the edge of the Tennessee River at Ross' Landing and overlooking a great expanse served as the main stage for the big name acts. More than fifty thousand attended the show. The blanket of people up and down the banks of the river proved this to be quite accurate indeed. The day came, and I had my tech rehearsal, getting the lights and cues set, the sound level right (I now used music to accompany many of my skits now, helping me time out my show better), and the general feel for the stage. Still hours away from show time, the activity remained around the general festival and had not begun to gravitate to watch the concert.

About an hour before my performance, the stage manager instructed me to use the houseboat that had just been tied to the back of the barge. With my costume and makeup bag in tow, I boarded the floating makeup room. Crystal Gayle also used it as a dressing room as it turned out, although not aboard at the time. Looking around and seeing her clothes and dresses for the show laid out neatly lifted my anticipation to a higher level. In reality getting ready would be no different than any other show, first the face and then the costume. Only now preparation included a few minutes to calm down. Going out on the deck of the houseboat and doing some simple stretching to loosen up also mitigated the nerves a bit. Coming off the boat and making my way to the stage, Crystal Gayle and I were introduced. She wished me luck, and I, in turn, thanked her for the opportunity.

Typically not one to get nervous, excitement is the best way to describe my pre-show state of mind. This time, admittedly, it proved difficult not to think about the crowd too much. Sunset descended on the mass of people as the stage went black signaling my entrance onstage. The spotlights beamed directly on me as the music started. A surreal sense washed over me producing a brief thought of how strangely foreign this experience felt. The show began with my back to the audience (that will be explained shortly on how that came to be), consciously focused intentions on sending electric waves of energy to the back of the crowd and faintly aware my legs quivered ever so slightly when they were normally rock-solid. This lasted for a few seconds, but I certainly noticed the adrenaline until settling my attention to the performance itself, turning smoothly to face the crowd with a committed focus, snapping into what had been done hundreds of times before; and the strangely foreign feeling gave way to a sense of joy. After my forty minutes onstage, the sun had disappeared; and taking my bow, I now experienced the wonderfully massive sound of cheers and applause. On only a few occasions did I ever prolong a bow to soak it in, but here was one of those moments which produced the contented wave of warmth in those extra few seconds. (To my recollection the others were at my high school and UNCSA and one other hometown performance.)

Once exiting offstage left, I turned to watch the crowd hear Crystal's introduction through the massive sound system as the fifty thousand roared with approval. She made her way on from right wing of the stage. I watched her for a few songs and then returned to the houseboat to change into my street clothes choosing not to return to the offstage area. After my biggest performance, the show completed. With no one to share in my personal achievement and not knowing what else to do, I just left, grabbing my suitcase and gear, deciding to head for my hotel room. Walking through the crowd as they listened to the headliner sing couldn't be avoided. People were everywhere.

Many people recognized me (partly because of my ubiquitous presence at the festival throughout the week) and complimented my performance, with one of those accolades coming from the very farthest seating area. It is that one comment, not to diminish the others, that made me look back to the stage where I had just given my all and notice how amazingly far away the stage appeared, and still my actions translated the entire distance. Thanking those who congratulated me, but not stopping, the mile-long stroll back to my room continued. After showering, changing, and a quick dinner, I made my way to a private party given by the festival organizers. B. B. King sat down and started playing his guitar for the limited gathering, where I found myself sitting off to his side a mere six feet away. This is as good as a day could get and one to remember, and there would not be another quite like it again. Though many fine days fill my memories, this one stands out.

In the inventiveness of the actor-mime and in his expression is revealed the comic and tragic depth of his art; this inventiveness is itself linked to the knowledge of life or, in other words, to the observation of a man among his fellow men. (Marcel Marceau)

1984: New York with Marcel Marceau to the New Orleans World's Fair

Marcel Marceau first appeared on *The Ed Sullivan Show* and *The Tonight Show Starring Johnny Carson* in the late 1950s and early 1960s. *The Ed Sullivan Show* came on at 8:00 p.m. Sunday evening. It seemed that everyone watched. We were no different, and it was when I remember seeing Marcel for the first time. I remember seeing him many times on Johnny Carson, but don't recall the first time. When Marcel had been slated to perform live at the War Memorial Building in Trenton, New Jersey (a huge venue seating a few thousand), in January 1975, I grabbed the opportunity. Somehow I made it backstage after the show by hanging around the edge of the stage and telling someone I studied mime and asking if I could meet Mr. Marceau. He invited me and my parents, who also went to the show, to come meet him backstage. After a brief introduction, with me explaining to him I studied mime, he reached for my program giving me his autograph with an inscription in my program, not merely a scribbled signature. I told Marcel of the classes in New York with Claude Kipnis and his troupe members Rudy Benda and Doug Day, when I attended the American Academy of Dramatic Arts in 1973. We had a brief conversation about that. He encouraged me to keep learning the craft. Yet, the thing that I will never forget is how gentle and kind he came across, unrushed although still in his white-face makeup and costume, also shaking hands with my mother and father. This lasted for only four or five minutes at most, but made a deep impression on me, as you can see. In 1984 I had the privilege to study with him in New York while he was in the USA.

At the beginning of the first class, I spoke with Marcel about our meeting in Trenton and how much it meant to me then. With a smile he thanked me for the saying so, knowing he had most likely forgotten that momentary introduction. I then reminded him about my work with Claude Kipnis and some of his troupe members, Rudy Benda and Doug Day. Claude had died suddenly a short time earlier from cancer, and he asked me when was the last time I had seen Claude. Whether this triggered his memory of our having met or not, I found that as he had asked me about Claude, Marcel had looped his arm into my arm turning me away from the class leading me across the studio room floor diagonally from one corner to the other. Walking arm in arm, this separated us from the rest of the class, as they stood clustered watching us go off to the other end of the long, narrow, windowed on one side and mirrored on the other, New York studio. He had his arm draped across my shoulder as I recalled to him the last time I saw Claude. I told Marcel that we met by chance in front of the Bijou Theatre where Mummenschanz (a mime show) was performing in New York during the fall of 1979, about a year before Claude died. It was a bit cold because I remember complimenting the coat Claude wore. Claude and I had a nice chat about what was going on in our current careers that I went on to the North Carolina School of the Arts in Winston-Salem and studied mime with James Donlon and Bob Francesconi and graduated with a Bachelor of Fine Arts degree that year and was back in New York working on- an off-Broadway play. Briefly chatting for maybe five minutes, we wished each other luck, said our goodbyes, and went our ways. Marcel asked me if I could discern that Claude showed any signs of ill-health because of the cancer and if I knew of his suffering at that time. I responded that he really did not appear much different to my eye. Claude had died in February of 1981 of cancer. At this point, we were face-to-face as he stood very close, while we spoke in almost hushed voices. Absorbing any information I could offer, Marcel seemed to take his focus off my eyes. Slowly changing his gaze from my eyes to out beyond me, he pivoted gently while staring off and then up. His body rotated away from me; and as he turned, he simultaneously said to me, with a quizzically plaintive contemplation, "Death—a very strange phenomenon!"

Without another word, I believe he pondered how he could translate that into his work. Remaining alone I stood in the corner of the room, while he gently, seemingly, glided away. Marcel was about ten feet away from me and about thirty feet away from rejoining class when something like a power surge hit me in the chest. I stood watching his back as this power burst jolted me with some force. It has been said that when someone of stature is in a room, there is an energy that pervades the entire room. This occurs with actors on the stage or performers or even politicians. I have felt that type of energy before and since, but never experienced that kind of invisible thrust from someone walking away from me.

Once I rejoined the class across the room from this very warm and personal interaction with Marcel, they asked me what we talked about because they said when Marcel turned around to walk back, he seemed so far away in thought. They remarked about feeling a difference in the energy in the room. This very powerful moment in my life had a definite effect on me. From that point on, I started nearly each one of my mime shows with my back facing the audience and concentrating on sending out an energy wave to the last row of the theater.

And being a mime, I search for the words of what the time spent in his classes meant to me. And there really aren't that many. Some things in life defy satisfactory description. Now being a professional mime and touring the USA with my solo mime show *Body, Mime, and Soul* for a number of years by this point, his teachings taught me much but reaffirmed so much more.

As much as I enjoyed and learned from Marcel Marceau, credit must be given here to the man who influenced my mime career the most. James Donlon, a professional mime from California, taught for a time at the North Carolina School of the Arts and influenced me greatly. His classes were exciting and fun, if you enjoy working hard anyway. They involved movement, masks, props, commedia dell'arte, and other periods of theater. These classes were only a part of our training, as I mentioned earlier, but they were instrumental in how I approached theater from then on and still draw upon lessons that we learned. Great classes taught by one of the most proficient mimes in the world, Donlon knows that I got much from him but doubts he knows how tremendously thankful I am to this day for his influence.

The Reset Button: Going Back Home to Regroup

The 1984 New Orleans World Exposition, the World's Fair, could not attract enough visitors. Money started drying up, and when that happened, the first things to go were the entertainers. I happened to end up one of those casualties. When the choice came to stick it out in New Orleans without a job or to pack it in to regroup at my parent's home in New Jersey, I headed north. My folks split their year by living in New Jersey in the warm months and going to Florida the other half of the year. July in New Orleans left me flat as it finished my relationship with Barb. Mom and Dad welcomed me back, allowing me to get things on an even keel. My schedule had me going out on tour a few times in the coming months, so getting back to New Jersey provided me with familiar surroundings and a great place to continue on. When winter came, I had the beach house to myself. During this time, to make ends meet, taking a couple of restaurant jobs filled in the gaps. Lavallette is a seasonal beach town. Finding the best opportunities meant switching jobs when needed.

Professionally things were going along at a steady pace; and now I tried to use any extra time to retool my show, adding skits and music and fabricating banners and props. Living home again had its benefits giving me the break needed and the time to consider my options. Do I get back into New York? Continuing to book shows and staying busy led me to the answer. My show still trended upward, and leaving it now, when there could be a breakthrough, kept me on the mime path. With each passing season, hope renewed in getting to that big advance forward. The giant wave I worked toward never really came although my bookings increased, keeping me in the constant state of hope. There would be no shortcuts. So many times it felt like such an arduous task, only to be refreshed by a great show or a wonderful tour. The tours and shows were the rewards of the process. There's no question that an enormous amount of work went into touring, but the joy of performing cushioned the tough times. Schools were having me for return visits, and new ones were coming on board, with a few residency programs and master classes thrown in. On top of that, my reviews were all consistently positive which added that boost of encouragement. Flying to gigs now and then, with each payday increasing, my career felt like it had shifted up. At this point making up to $2000 a night, nothing dissuaded me from thinking I traveled the correct path.

Here is part of a review from the University of Miami:

He didn't say much but said a lot.

Mime Ken Alcorn was rewarded by an enthusiastic standing ovation at the Lakeside Dessert Cafe's inaugural performance Sunday evening.

150-plus students gathered in a café-style atmosphere—complete with soft candlelight---and sat out the cold weather for Alcorn's show.

The mime started with a simple dance to the tune of Earth, Wind and Fire's "Fantasy" and from there his show grew into a funny, involving and sometimes provocative presentation.

His view of the birth of a baby and its growth into manhood held the audience's attention and provided some interesting reflections of the world around us.

For example, at the start of the piece, Alcorn took a fetal position and worked his way out of the womb. When he stuck his head out and saw what was around him, he quickly went back to the security inside.

Perhaps the evening's funniest segment was "Masks," a piece which gave the audience a look at some very different and very funny characters.

Other pieces ranged from the romantic and thought-provoking "Romance" to the lively and humorous "The Tortoise and the Hare."

"Romance," which Alcorn portrayed, using only his hands, was delicately done with smooth hand motions. Though, at times, they lacked subtlety. Yet "Romance's" gentle, almost consoling tone

benefitted from Alcorn's precise choreography and execution.

On a lighter note, his rendition of the classic race between tortoise and hare brought laughter from the audience.

By using quick limb movements such as shaking his legs to represent the energetic hare while making slow and tedious moves for the tortoise, Alcorn did a good job of differentiating the two competitors. At the same time, he created a light, funny version of the children's tale.

The most amazing quality of Alcorn's show is that he said nothing. At times he let out a few words, only to fetch them back, knowing that mimes aren't supposed to talk. Unlike a comedian, he can't rely on punch lines or accents to get the humor across. Alcorn's show was purely visual.

And with those visuals, he evoked emotion in his audience. As a mime, he relied on the basics of human perception and, without saying a word, brought an energy and electricity to the stage that would normally require a lot of extras.

The University of Miami Student Entertainment Committee deserves a note of commendation, not only for taking a risk in doing something totally new on campus, but making it a success. (Juan Carlos Coto and Tony Fins, The Miami Hurricane, March 4, 1986)

CHAPTER

7

TRANSITIONS

The Flat Tire, the Bride, and the Ride toward the Sunset

Body, Mime, and Soul started with a simple prodding and gentle demand to assemble a show. Because of this, New York had faded to a distant memory. This choice made, there seemed to be no turning back now for I had now traveled long down this road, still dreaming and envisioning a way to parlay this experience into an acting career someday. It existed only as a wish at this point since no set date determined when I would make the transition. It remained just one far off option.

Returning to perform at the Foxcroft School, another all-girls prep school in Northern Virginia, brought me back to the one of the original five where it all had begun. Many schools invited me back every other year or so for an engagement. The Friday night show went well. I spent the night in the guest quarters. Quite often the private schools would have a guest suite on the campus to stay in instead of my staying at a motel. In the morning I headed to town for an early start home.

Middleburg, Virginia, is in the heart of horse country at the very north of it, in the shadow of the Blue Ridge Mountains, and where I'd go to cash my performance check, learning early on in the touring game that cashing checks on the bank they were written on, if available, would save me a lot of waiting for the funds to clear. I traveled with a bank deposit bag, one that banks provide or used to provide the local businesses for their deposits. It would usually come with the bank's name printed on it with the zipper on top. By the end of the tours, this bag often bulged. On one hand I felt a bit like Scrooge and, on the other, a bit like Bob Cratchit. One got to keep the money, and the other only could count it. It's almost the same feeling you get when, as a young kid, your dad hands you a stack of money to count and hold. It's yours for that moment, but you know it's about to leave your hands very, very soon. With bills to pay, I sadly, never got to hold it very long.

Now with the banking out of the way, I returned to the car to discover a flat tire. With the sun gleaming down on this beautiful spring morning, my jacket came off, sleeves were rolled up, and tire changing commenced. I hoped it only to be a nail hole requiring an inexpensive patch and not a costly replacement. All this fun while shipwrecked on the main street in front of an art gallery in the very center of town threw my schedule off. Once the tire had been changed, though, a gentleman working in the art gallery had observed the situation and kindly came to offer me the use of his restroom to wash my hands. *What a nice thing to recognize*, I thought. A simple gesture such as this can change the tenor of a mood instantly, as it did with me. Hands now clean, making my way back to the front of the gallery, after thanking him, I glanced over the fine art displayed all around. A very lovely woman walked in just then, and they greeted each other. Then he turned and politely introduced Jan to me. During our conversation, Jan mentioned that a flat tire to her car delayed her making some scheduled appointment. What a coincidence! We both were not in the places we intended, thwarted by flat tires bringing about this fated meeting. This led to our having lunch before my return to New Jersey that afternoon. The following weekend, a drive back to Virginia for a date might have appeared crazy. I didn't think twice about it.

June saw me up and down the road for shows and NACA meetings, stopping once again on my way back through Virginia. Jan had a painting on the easel she wanted to finish; so she set up a blank gesso-covered Masonite board, handed me some brushes, squeezed oil paint onto a pallet, and told me to start painting. Purple, yellow, black, and white paint, mixed in just the right way, produced an interesting abstract nude. (Years later, it sold at auction for $2.00.) Before I met her, she had owned an art store but now painted in different mediums for a living. Maybe because she happened to be an artist, her belief in my artistic journey resonated with me, quite like being validated. These were carefree, light, and joyful times filled with exploring art together.

We impulsively decided to marry soon into our relationship and did so in January of 1987. This tended to be more an emotional decision than a logical one, yet I moved to Virginia and found a job selling pianos for Jordan Kitt's Music. The scanty bookings of my mime show reflected fewer shows that spring, and the fall season was still too far off to know what to expect. Selling pianos wasn't the problem. The mall's retail hours had us closing at 9:30 p.m., getting home an hour or so later. Weekends in retail sales are pretty much mandatory, and the newlyweds didn't see much of each other.

Jan accompanied me to a performance scheduled at The University of Delaware. She traveled with me from time to time. As she had on quite a few occasions before. The university provided the lobby of the main building for my show, situated so it allowed students to walk right in front of the stage to pass through. Either that or they would have to circle around behind the audience, and that would be inconvenient, so few chose that. There was no theatrical lighting, and the platforms they furnished were dreadfully too small and not more than a foot off of the floor. In other words, it's an abysmal set of circumstances to perform (just about as bad as performing in front of the cafeteria crowd at lunch time). I could have been a tree and gotten more attention. Few people cared to stop to watch, only for a few minutes or so, if at all. My first act which usually lasted forty-five to fifty minutes clocked out in record time, done in about twenty. I cut pieces out deeming it senseless to do them. At one point I looked to the back of the room and saw Jan with the most pitiful expression of empathy, a look that seemed to ask, "Why are you putting yourself through this?"

Desperation must have been kicking in, to the point that, during that fall, I even flew out to Peoria, Iowa, to meet with an owner of a booking agency who expressed interest in representing my show. At this point, we decided it might be a good idea to have someone else handling that, allowing me to concentrate on the artistic side. Maybe this would rejuvenate the tour. He told me he would introduce me to some producers and investors. In meeting them, we could work out the details to expand my show with a traveling set and lighting equipment. Sadly, he wasted my time and money. There were no investors, and he turned out to be a fraud. When I confronted him, he tried to pacify my anger with the offer of drugs and women. What bothered me most was being completely deceived by this guy. On the next available flight home, I concluded that, in truth, the only things lost were a couple of days and a few bucks.

With the trailing off of the bookings, coupled with the past couple of miserable experiences, the time to adjust my vision for the future had arrived. Fighting windmills, as with Don Quixote, took on the same weariness as I booked fewer shows. Periodically, there would be a string of performances together again, but the long tours were over and the sunset came upon me without pity. After Christmas of that year, I took an eight-to-five job with US Sprint.

The gem cannot be polished without
friction nor man without trials.
-Confucius

Painting and Writing Music

Painting had opened another expression for me to tap into, and because that was my brother's domain and his excellence, it never occurred to me that anything I produced would ever compare in any way to his art, so I stayed away from it. Jan encouraged me to pick up the brush. With her own studio and supplies, she worked predominantly in oils these days. Although an expert in other mediums as well, at least at this stage of her life, oil paints were her focus. It did not matter to her that what I painted lacked any semblance of technique in the beginning. Her encouragement inspired me, possibly because it brought out something different in me.

At one point I shared a group of paintings with my brother and asked him what he thought. Bob viewed them and without hesitation looked me in the eye and asked, "What do you think of them?"

"I think they're pretty good!" I said hoping he would agree.

"Then that is all that matters! It makes no difference what I think or anyone else thinks. If *you* are pleased with your work and you did your best, nothing anyone says, including me, should make you think otherwise," he responded in a very big brotherly way.

Bob may not remember that moment, but it meant the world to me. I did not need his approval for my paintings. In his loving way he refused to criticize when he could very well have. Bob has no trouble giving me a sharp elbow to my ego now and then, like big brothers can do. By not cutting into the work, it fell on me to be the judge and jury of my art. This spilled over into all of the areas of my creativity.

I enjoy painting and think a few really good ones came out, but many things got in the way of doing it on a continuing basis. There are still paintings inside of me that will eventually be brushed.

Jan decided she did not want married life and left the marriage. I didn't see that one coming. I got hit by a bolt out of the blue. This departure didn't happen because she didn't love me or that I didn't love her. She just came to a place in her life that she did not want marriage. We had a wonderful romance which possibly should have stayed just as that. Getting married fit part of a big beautiful dream.

She woke up from the dream a lot sooner than I did maybe. It did feel like a truck hit me and then backed up again.

Hiding from the emotions and truth of this abrupt change couldn't be ignored. Wishing this away would not happen. This wasn't my first relationship to end. Knowing I had survived the past ones, things eventually would be alright, but this hit me like a blow to the gut. I needed to get my breath back.

We left each other on gentle terms, but even so, my broken heart would take time to repair. Music and writing and work helped fill the time to do so, as it always did.

Another Reset Button

In trying to make money the traditional way working for US Sprint, where I sold business phone plans, the tedium just about sucked any life I had left in me right down the toilet. Depression and deep despondency did not mix well with sales either. After two months of this, I, once again, found my way back to a job waiting tables in a restaurant while playing the piano in another, still booking my mime show, but just not as many. My immediate goal now shifted to get my life together. The impact of what I considered a failed marriage set me back, more of a shock to my system than a loss of confidence. For a short while this would make me a bit tentative and careful not to make decisions without a lot more thought.

A quaint restaurant in Purcellville, Virginia, named Aufdenberg's hired me to wait tables. The Hamilton Garden Inn, just up the road, hired me to play cocktail piano on the weekends. Shortly after starting work, Jerry Aufdenberg expanded his restaurant, creating a separate bar area, and added bartending to my schedule there as well. Most of us who worked and played there seemed to be all repairing from some miserable experience and trying to get through it. It became a hangout for a time, a little window of time. We called the place, lovingly, "The House of the Broken Toys" referring to our collective problems.

One night, August 1, 1988, to be precise, while I worked the restaurant side, a very attractive lady came in for dinner with her parents; and to my good fortune, they were seated in my section. We were not particularly busy at the time giving us a chance to chat. Preparing a Caesar salad for them tableside allowed the conversation with them to develop, all while I tossed the romaine. They were in town because the young lady, Beth, was opening up her medical practice in the next couple of days. Her mother and father were there to celebrate the event with her. I called her the next day after offering to show her around the area. We met for a cup of coffee and then went to the library to get our library cards. Pretty romantic, don't you think so? And although I wasn't exactly looking for romance or a relationship, it seemed a good idea to keep an open mind. She was nice and really cute, and even if it turned out to be mild interest, her attention soothed my bruised and repairing ego. My divorce papers still hadn't come through, so a new commitment did not figure in as part of my current plans.

Beth disappeared for a month and then one night reappeared in the bar. Serving her a glass of wine, as the usual friends gathered that night, I introduced Beth to everyone. She had much to do in opening her office, so it didn't seem odd that she hadn't come in for a while. It turned out that in addition to setting up her office nearby, she also found the time to break up with her current boyfriend, thereby clearing the deck for me I prefer to think.

We enjoyed talking, and she dropped in every few nights as time would allow. About the third or fourth time she came in, one of the other bartenders leaned over and asked, "So has Ken asked you to the wedding?"

"No, he hasn't. What wedding?" Beth asked.

"Lee and Kim's. They're getting married in a couple of weeks. Would you like to go with me?" I asked now feeling fully obligated to.

Beth said yes. I consider that our first official date. On the wedding day, the happy couple left the ceremony of the outdoor event by floating away in a hot air balloon. Kim threw the bridal bouquet from the basket as it ascended above the rooftop. The flowers plummeted directly into my arms. At the same time Lee tossed the garter down as well. This just drifted down also landing in my hand, sealing my fate forever I figured. My divorce papers came a few days later. I hardly wanted to rush into a relationship. This one just evolved as we spent more and more time together.

Marvin Moore, the vice president of Jordan Kitt's Music, called me about returning to work selling pianos, this time in the warehouse location and not in a mall. Accepting this very stable job at a time where essentially my mime career slowed down dramatically felt like a right move. Working in the restaurants was a stopgap measure. At the time, I considered very strongly returning to New York for another go at it. That would mean, in all likelihood, giving up on a new developing relationship with Beth. Taking the job selling pianos gave me time to give our relationship a chance. If it did not work out, New York would still be there.

Mime provided a great platform for me to do what I did well. It also declined in its appeal as time went on. After a decade of traveling, the luster diminished, and mime descended out of favor, pushed to the side by stand-up comics who would use us as fodder for their punch lines. Mimes were and still are, to some extent, an easy laugh to a stand-up. To be fair, many street mimes gave the art form a bad name too by being quite mediocre and simplistic. Just putting on whiteface makeup and pulling an imaginary rope or making an invisible box did not make you an accomplished mime. They became rampant. This caused the comics to use us as target practice. After all, what were the mimes going to say in defense? Would we just stand there and say nothing? Who spoke up for us? There were no words for this type of thing. The comics had the platform and used it.

Like all good things, my mime time had reached its prime and now faded away. And though I still did an occasional show, the bell had rung, making it necessary to make changes.

By the time my mime career dwindled away, for all intents and purposes, the mime years had seen me living from New Jersey to Dothan, Alabama, to New Orleans, back to New Jersey, and then to Northern Virginia that included multiple addresses. This created an almost military lifestyle of constant moving, something that has never really stopped in any regard. None of this seemed abnormal in any way because I had so many friends who traveled the college circuit. This just became a way of life. Honing my skills and always hoping the next door opened could be the one that launched my career to the next level justified my thinking along these lines. That may have happened to some, but it became apparent as things went along after all the years and miles spent on this pursuit that the college circuit was its own reward. Very few lifted above that to any great heights.

Now, conversely, being an entertainer already well known having achieved a level of fame already would enhance their reputation by doing the college tour. By that celebrity status, they could make quite a bit of money from the big university concerts. Coming from being an unknown talent, finding a way to break in made the process a little more daunting, not impossible at all, but certainly a longer road to travel typically.

It had become evident that if I were to continue with this type of life, there would be no prospect of a normal home life of marriage, and family would not be in the equation. Relationships had already been ended by choosing to seek fame and fortune instead of building a future together or a solid stable income. Living job to job, not in a place to be able to commit to any of that unless something happened thrusting me into the limelight providing a more stable income, those things would only be dreams.

Better a witty fool than a foolish wit.
(Feste in *Twelfth Night*, Shakespeare)

Twelfth Night

Ambitions give us hope. Hope raises our faith. Faith gives us courage. Courage gives us strength.

Beth and I married almost two years after we met. During those two years, Beth's practice got busier. I helped her in her office, leaving piano sales behind. Our relationship flowed very gently through this time. I knew things were changing. Meeting Beth saw to that.

The opportunity to play Feste in *Twelfth Night* presented itself when a local theater company, Elden Street Players in Herndon, Virginia, cast me in the role. The company had already established a great reputation. I had wanted to play this character since playing Fabian, a smaller role, fifteen years before as a member of The Bucks County Playhouse Repertory Company. For the first time in ten years, I would have a speaking role. Feste is not the easiest part to memorize. Shakespeare is difficult enough; but to say lines written to sound nonsensical when they actually make a great deal of sense, in a language that, although it is English, is foreign to our modern ear, posed a huge challenge which added to the enjoyment immensely. My fellow actors turned out to be tremendously accomplished and a tremendous pleasure to work with. The newspaper critiques were positive, again, giving me the encouragement and reassurance that I hadn't lost my skill. Don't let anyone kid you. Getting a good review means something. Consider the source, enjoy the nice things said, and do not dwell on the negative ones. Give them a thought and move on. Fix it if it needs fixing. Smile if they don't. I am usually harder on myself than any critic is anyway.

Shift of Focus

Some turning points are well defined at the outset. Some are identified by the prism of time. Transitions sometimes occur in stages, and looking back, a new trajectory had begun. I had entered into a completely different phase of my life.

Beth needed some help in the back office of her practice, so I stepped into a job that I had no formal training for, one which would lead me to places I would never have dreamt.

Working in the back office of Beth's medical practice allowed me to be with her and learn a new part of life that I had very little interaction with previously. Life in a medical office taught me of a world I knew very little about. The amount of reading needed just to understand the paperwork introduced me to a job unlike any other position I had held to this point, and fascinating too. Being able to help build her business by understanding the inner workings of a medical practice would, I found, be valuable. Since this didn't come close to my sphere of reference before, Beth could now talk to me about her business without her words falling on completely ignorant ears when there happened to be a matter to discuss. But since I acquired the terminology in that area, nodding my head with a look of complete understanding, even though much flew high over my head, allowed me to at least strive to grasp her world. What astounds me to this day is how she retains and recalls the vast data bank of medical terminology. Never mind knowing how to pronounce it all.

We both knew that this would be a temporary situation. Having experience in an office might lead to a better situation down the road. For now, though, this demonstrated my commitment to support her new practice.

Marriage did not change my working in Beth's office, but the arrival of our son did. It made more sense to have someone stay home with Jamie, hiring someone else for the office than to have a nanny. Again, neither of us intended my working in her office to be a long-term proposition and never had been.

"Hello, Dolly!" 1971 from left to right, Carole
Appleget, Ken Alcorn, Carol Cope, Frank Smith.

The School's first production of 'The Threepenny Opera,' directed by Robert Murray, in 1978. A second production will be presented April 20-23. L-R: Carol Drake, Ken Alcorn, Jay Corlough, Billy Moize Jr., Mark Hough, R. Gary Simpson, Robert Hoshour (Gary Lauderdale on table)

The Threepenny Opera, 1978, Ken Alcorn as Mack The Knife

Ken as MacHeath,(Mack the Knife) in Threepenny Opera,
From left to right, Bob Hoshour, Matt Ashford, Samantha Daniels,
Julie Luker, George Altman, Carol Drake, Ken Alcorn, Kevin Barrows

Ken Alcorn, as Winfield Davis, 1978 in
Indulgences in a Louisville Harem.

Ken Alcorn as Winfield Davis, Richard Gardner as the
Professor, 1978 in Indulgences in a Louisville Harem.

Ken Alcorn head shot by Larry Lapidus, New York, 1979

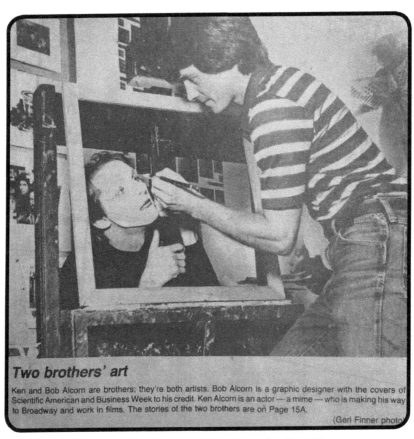

Two brothers' art

Ken and Bob Alcorn are brothers; they're both artists. Bob Alcorn is a graphic designer with the covers of Scientific American and Business Week to his credit. Ken Alcorn is an actor — a mime — who is making his way to Broadway and work in films. The stories of the two brothers are on Page 15A.

(Geri Finner photo)

Ken And Bob Alcorn, 1980, picture by Geri Finner

Happy mask

Uh-Oh mask

Lowery Steinbald functional object mask. Stolen 1981. R.I.P.

Ken Alcorn staged the production "Body, Mime, and Soul" at Kennesaw College on February 24. Above is one of his visual stunts.

Photo by Max Tate

Ken Alcorn in performance of Body, Mime and Soul. 1981

Ken Alcorn, in performance with sousaphone. 1981

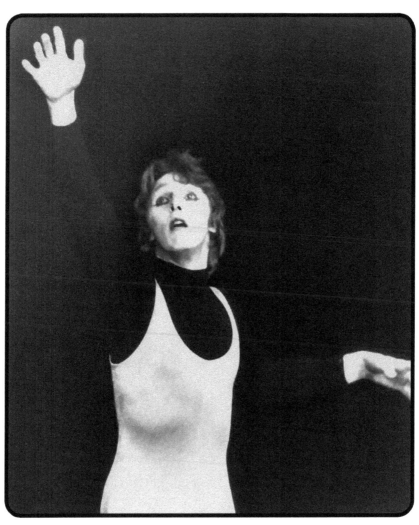

In performance Body, Mime and Soul 1982

Ken Alcorn- Mime 1985

Marcel Marceau by Ken Alcorn 1986

Beth on our wedding day

Jane and George Alcorn, Mom and Dad

Sousaphone and musical instrument fountain by Ken
Alcorn. This is the same sousaphone I performed with.

Beth and Ken's children, Jamie, Jeremy, Joshua and Jenna

CHAPTER
8

A New Direction:
Full time father

The Most Underrated Job in the World

Being a man in our society connotes certain images: workmen in work clothes carrying tools, businessmen in suits carrying briefcases, athletes wearing helmets and pads, servicemen in uniform, policemen in blue, cowboys on horseback, and any other professions that are easily identified by their regalia and equipment.

Women are now seen in the workforce doing and wearing the same as what I have just mentioned. This has become a way of life, where boundaries have relaxed and it is not uncommon to see women now holding what was traditionally viewed as men's jobs. Women now do anything that men have done. No one bats an eye to see a woman driving a semi, swinging a hammer, running a corporation, or holding a scalpel. I believe this to be wonderful, actually. If this is what a woman desires to do, who am I to oppose it?

Change happens over time, and as change comes new complications present themselves. With the options of having a two-income household (and not always an option but a necessity in many cases) come the pressures of added competition in the workforce, having more people available for many of the same jobs.

Our society has grown so rapidly with many of the traditional boundaries pushed through. Just as we have needed to recognize the undeniable abilities and talents of women joining the so-called man's work world, is it any wonder that the interchanging of jobs would occur having men become part of what has been recognized to be the woman's realm?

Take a man and put him in what has been a traditionally female role, such as a secretary, nurse, or hairdresser, for example, and watch society lift its collective eyebrow, tilt its collective head, and cross its collective arms in cynical apprehension. Even in this day and age, it is frowned upon to be seen doing typically traditional feminine roles or jobs not using muscle mass with men characterized as weak or impotent. Some of those perceptions have changed, I freely admit, since the 2008 depression forcing many to assume a different role.

Even still, have a man choose the role of a homemaker as a stay-at-home dad, and he will face the belittlement of his worthiness in the grand scheme of things, his being relegated to the sidelines in a man's company and excluded in the world of stay-at-home mothers.

"How can you say such things?" you may ask.

I am a stay-at-home father. For nearly twenty-five years, this has been my life. I speak with the authority of one man who has experienced the challenges of raising four children in a nontraditional way through a time when this choice has become more prevalent, but still looked down upon. There are not many books on this subject from a man's perspective, and I wish only to add mine. Maybe it will help to contribute in a way that promotes understanding and possibly recognition of some difficulties in a man's taking on this challenge.

The path to my becoming a stay-at-home father appeared in stages and then was considered with deliberation and, ultimately, chosen for a purpose. Obligation set this choice in motion, one that I felt very strongly about. My wife is a surgeon, as has been already stated. It made no sense for her to give up her career after thirteen years of preparation with a developing medical office growing to stay at home while I struggled to find a job that held no future guarantees. We looked at our marriage as a partnership and always have. Please understand that I did not raise our children alone. Although the traditional roles were switched, where Beth was the main source of income with me staying home with the children, both approached our positions as a team unit. This put pressure on Beth with the burden of being the provider, yet it also put pressure on me to put my ego and career aside. Both of these adjustments were not always a natural fit. They took work and understanding from each other.

While Beth actualized the dream that her thirteen years of intense education and training beyond high school produced, I had to undergo a mind-set transformation that would take me away from what my seven years of college and ten years of touring as a professional mime had given me. Again I changed course and adapted to a new set of circumstances. Could I have gone back to New York or gone to Hollywood? That choice was off the table now. It would have been a foolish folly to even entertain the thought now. Besides being a husband and a father, location and Beth's job held us in place, making that kind of career choice moot, unless other sacrifices were made. Being a father from a distance or one where the schedule required an erratic home life did not interest me. The scar from my first marriage reminded me that I did not want to go through a repeated pain of a divorce. To turn away from my obligations of fatherhood would not be an option either. This demanded nothing less than a full commitment to both stations, in my view. I embraced the commitment to Beth during our courtship and marriage. We planned on having a family, so marriage and family took precedence which took on a fixed mind-set the day we said, "I do."

Birth

Jamie was born only a few months before my turning thirty-eight years old. I knew people who were grandparents by this time in their lives. No matter, excitement does not have an age requirement. On the day Jamie arrived, I remember the exuberance, a most spectacular feeling and one that words cannot fully capture. In the couple of weeks before Beth's due date, Jamie decided to turn himself around in her womb, placing himself upside down. His legs were situated with his heels next to his head and his butt positioned in the birth canal where his head should be. This is called a frank breech position. I just called it "bass-ackward." Anyway, the OB-GYN tried to correct this by doing what is called an external version, which is a maneuver performed by trying to turn the baby into proper position by gently pushing the baby from the outside. This procedure made no difference. Jamie entrenched himself in this position with his legs straight up next to his head, in a clothespin position, which prevented the turn. Had he been just breech, a turn would have likely been successful because his legs would not have been extended out. He then would be able to do the somersault that would have returned him to a proper birth position. This condition, in our case, led to the conclusion that a Caesarian section be performed.

Many men may not have the opportunity to observe the birth of a child, but nowadays many more will. If the option is there to witness this, I highly recommend it. This is an awesomely remarkable event. I share some of my thoughts and experiences of our first child being born, for a couple of reasons: firstly, because of the wonder of it and, secondly, because of the bond I experienced with both Beth and the baby. Not every birth, sadly, comes without risk. Let me tell you a bit of what transpired.

The decision of the C-section was made the day before the scheduled delivery date.

Knowing the delivery needed to be done by C-section left me with mixed emotions. Anxiousness held my attention until overridden by anticipation. Of course, no one wanted to see Beth go through a surgery. It came with a longer recovery time and involved more pain. The frank breech position of the baby took a vaginal birth off the table, so to speak, taking the risk to mother and child away, at least the dangers that were present because of that position.

Fathers are now routinely in the room when their baby is being born, not so for a C-section. Maybe because I am a husband of a doctor, the OB-GYN extended the privilege to me. I am not sure, but if I could be in the room, I wanted to be there.

We arrived at the hospital just after one o'clock. The doctor made one more attempt at the external version to turn the baby around, hoping to avoid surgery, all to no avail. The nurses wired Beth up to all sorts of monitors and gadgets to check whatever they needed to keep track of. When the anesthesiologist came in to give

Beth an epidural, he turned to me and asked if I would like to sit down while he administered it. I said I was fine, not knowing why he would ask me that. He then produced a needle about a foot long and began to insert it into Beth's lower back. At this sight, I felt a bit wobbly. Sitting down now suddenly seemed an absolutely fine idea. Now I knew why he asked that.

I donned the required surgical outfits including hat mask and shoe coverings. The gloves were last to go on just before we entered the surgery room. After a short waiting period for the epidural to take effect, we rolled Beth to the operating room, and I grabbed my camera. After putting the gloves on, I took my place over Beth's left shoulder as she lay on the gurney in the fashion of a cross, with her arms extended out to both sides and the monitors all purring away. While all involved prepared, the glorious orange and red glow of the sky at sunset shone in through the windows, the brilliant sun magically pushed down by the profusion of color, magnificently accompanied by the music of Mozart's "Eine Kleine Nachtmusik." A small curtain erected halfway up her torso to shield Beth from watching gave me the choice to watch or not. For the incision, I chose not to. Instead I readied my camera to take pictures of the baby once he appeared. Intending not to show the graphic operation but only the baby, I carefully achieved just that by waiting for Jamie to be fully visible. In one of the best pictures I ever took, I captured Jamie taking his first breath, his feet up next to his ears, with the surgical lamp lighting his entry into the world surrounded by a multitude of blue-gloved hands and being held by our doctor. This took only seconds, and the curtain was gently lowered so Beth could see her beautiful baby boy.

Someone had told me to always stay with the baby during this process (to insure there is no switcheroo I imagine), so I stepped over with the nurses to the bassinette watching as they sponged Jamie clean and wrapped him in his first blanket. Because of the frank breech, his little legs stood straight out from being in the position for that length of time. In that blanket, he looked like a triangle with a head or a wedge of cheese. The possibility of hip problems later on could be one of the ramifications, but thankfully there were none. His legs lowered to normal over the next few days.

The stitches parallel to her beltline and the pain that came along with them limited Beth's movement. This included holding the baby comfortably to feed. Instead of breastfeeding, which for Beth was relatively difficult, we went right to formula. Breastfeeding when Beth returned to work would also be a challenge. We looked at breast pumps and even bought one, but the brochure made it look a lot easier than it turned out to be. The pamphlet depicted a lovely woman dressed in a business suit, talking on the phone while writing in a book with her jacket and blouse pulled wide open and two breast pump apparatuses attached to her nipples. Of course, she was smiling broadly. I can tell you Beth never used the phone, wrote in a book, or smiled while struggling to keep the suction pumps attached producing a modicum of milk. Within two days this pump quickly found its way back to the box to join the how-to pamphlet never to be heard from again.

We agreed that Beth would feed the baby for the late-night to midnight feeding and I would get up for the 4:00 a.m. feeding giving her a stretch of time of uninterrupted sleep. This is the pattern we used from then on. If there was a crying baby, I answered the call. Beth learned to sleep through that. I could not. This allowed her to be fresh for the office once she returned to work. But when the phone rang, Beth was upshot in bed and alert for a potential emergency call while I generally slept through that. It's interesting how our subconscious delineates priorities in our response mechanisms.

I learned that when the baby slept, it was wise for me to grab a nap, if I could. If not, housework, laundry, dishes, vacuuming, or whatever else pulled me kept things moving.

For a short while I continued to work a few hours a day in the office and would set up a portable crib during this time lasting a couple of months. After that I stayed home with Jamie.

The Growing Family and Faith

Jeremy was born eighteen months later with none of the issues that we dealt with during Jamie's delivery. It was a normal delivery, only this time I watched the entire astounding process, but once again astonished at the miracle of birth. The exuberance gave way eventually, tempered by the new dance and juggling routine of changing diapers, feeding schedules, laundry, and shopping, leading to more diapers, more feedings, cooking, doing dishes, and vacuuming. These were all parts of my days now. Two boys increased the job description exponentially. The strollers, portable cribs, bottles, toys, formula, diaper bag, creams and zinc oxide ointment, powder, and extra baby clothes were now my tools of the trade. My arms, I remember, were always so tired by the end of the day from all the lugging and carrying.

I loved being with the boys. The new sleep cycle inspired me to fold my pillow so I could get twice as much sleep. It didn't work too well. We got used to being tired. Oh, sure it would get better after a few months but not much. Beth took call coverage with the hospital seven to ten days a month, meaning if the phone rang and she was needed for an emergency, she would have to go in to take care of the situation and see the patient. She would not need to be concerned about the home front when leaving the house for the hospital. In our early days together, it made sense to drive with her. I'd sit and read in the doctor's lounge, while she took care of the patient. Unfortunately, once the baby entered the picture, this became unfeasible. Watching Beth take off in the middle of the night to go stop someone's bleeding still instills a helpless feeling in me. This is something I have never really gotten used to. Now that the kids are older, I do go in with her from time to time. No matter, though, how I feel about any of this, immediate response to the call and follow-through is of paramount importance. It is never known in these situations whether this one particular call will be a matter of life and death. This responsibility is met each and every time with the same sense of gravity and urgency.

The days of walking out of the house with only the keys to the car were gone completely. Loading the boys for a car ride took preparation, from making sure I had the diaper bag stocked and bottles filled to the strollers, portable crib, wagon, or any other equipment required. The kids' car seats were always a hassle. Like I said earlier, it's a juggling act, and nothing said here is shockingly new for mothers everywhere.

Women, and I am generalizing here, grow up watching their mothers, as boys typically watch how their fathers do things. Men have a set of roles, and women have their own set of roles. Of course, there is crossover. That's not my point here. During my time growing up, the common arrangement had one parent working and the other staying home. This is my experience. Living through the 1960s and 1970s, many women entered the workforce, creating more divided job assignments at home. New considerations to the division of the home workload were being established with men sharing the chores as the women would help to earn the family income.

By the 1980s, the image of the 1950s stay-at-home mother doing housework in her pretty flowered dress, wearing pearls and high heels (as depicted on the television sitcoms), began to shift to an image of women gravitating to the workforce, wearing sleek skirted dress suits or uniforms pertaining to their new positions. Women were portrayed on television as competent and able to compete in what had been a man's domain. On the other side of the spectrum, men were now being denigrated and put down as buffoons, lazy, good-for-nothing incompetents, always fouling up, and risking everything on some lame-brained scheme that only an idiot could devise. The father model, if even part of the family scenario, was figuratively emasculated in the name of humor. Very few television shows would put men in a positive light. The rise of the stand-up comic would bring attention to the failings of men, by both men and women comedians. Yes, women are not completely immune to the character assaults. They take some verbal abuse too. By and large though, the image of an inept and blundering fool for a husband, even if well meaning, became the standard description of a man in today's society.

One of the definitions used to describe comedy is the gaining of or the losing of dignity. To elevate someone to a position or place where it is obvious they do not belong and to see someone of great stature groveling in the gutter are two broad examples.

The movie *Mr. Mom* with Michael Keaton back in 1983 gives you a great example of how men were perceived leaving the man's traditional world and entering the woman's traditional world. We laughed at his battling the learning curve in a job whose value had been underestimated. Anyone who has stayed at home raising children knows the rigor involved. This movie shed some light on the subject but did so at the expense of making a man seem totally clueless and undercutting the importance of the position.

Just as women are encouraged to take on the business world, so too should men be encouraged as homemakers, or at least not ostracized. These transitions do take time to evolve. Many are aware that men are taking on by choice or necessity the job description of a stay-at-home father.

On Guard

An inherent risk a married man faces as a full time father is the potential to place him in situations where temptation can sway better judgment. Certainly that exists in every work situation, and inappropriate behavior is not relegated to one province. What I am saying here is that a stay-at-home father has entered into the arena of women. Interaction is important and necessary. Women interact with women in solving problems about running the house and raising the children all the time. They too started as amateurs for the most part and might have had more training growing up, but still need to learn different techniques available to them. Collaboration also provides opportunities for children to get together for playtime. It is an important benefit. Friendships develop and are important.

Forming a friendship in this way for a man with other women, no matter how well meaning and innocent, can place strains on not just his marriage potentially, but the other parties involved as well. Putting all that I have worked for to get to this point in my life in jeopardy would be foolish. Nothing untoward even had to occur, and yet a seed of distrust can grow into something unmanageable with insinuation alone.

Another of my father's admonitions not only about this subject but life in general was "Don't put yourself in harm's way."

Going to another woman's home for coffee or calling other women to chitchat was off limits. I would call close friends to see if they could watch my kids from time to time. Even with an invitation, I would not go into their homes without her husband being there, not only out of respect for her and for her husband but respect for my wife. If we did want to get the children together, it would be at a local park or a fast-food restaurant that had a playground and always in a very public place. I would avoid driving alone with a woman, in her car or mine. Babysitters called home before I took them so that their parents knew they would be delivered safely and when, again protecting their reputation and also protecting mine. This is how I set my parameters.

It may sound rigid and uptight, maybe so. Casual relationships can intensify if conditions present themselves and are not checked. I hadn't always looked at how my place in a situation would be interpreted. Maybe I just grew up. Life complicates things enough. I don't need to be a party to an entanglement that destroys and tears apart lives.

The interesting thing is that at this time in my life, I had more to talk about with the women than I did with men. Other men would confess to me that they wish they could stay at home with the kids but in the next sentence would say it would drive them crazy.

To encourage them I say, "You could if you set it up that way and, yes, crazy is part of it!" Then I add smiling, "Be careful what you ask for. You might get it."

Now with two boys, we looked to the future wanting to build a new home in the country. In between diapers and bottles and during their naps, I handled paperwork, research, and phone calls that needed to be made through the construction process. Just because I stayed at home with the kids did not mean my days were not full. They were very full, and no two were ever the same. Part of the job description of a parent is to be flexible, adaptable, and pliable.

Instead of woodshop I signed up for home economics back in high school, knowing there would be more possibility of cooking than building lamps shaped like the state of New Jersey or shoe shine boxes. In retrospect, all knowledge is helpful in parenting. Learning never stops.

CHAPTER
9

BUSINESS OPPORTUNITIES AND RUNNING A FAMILY

A New Stretch

To top everything else going on in our lives, we became independent business owners in the Amway business. Through this, I received an excellent business education along the way. As we worked the business, attending many seminars, conferences, and business meetings, we saw thousands of people with a dream come together. Some built their business to a very high level. We reached a modest level of success with our main obstacle revolving around scheduling. Beth, because of her schedule, needed to be virtually tethered to the area one third of the time, and coming home to a growing family made it difficult for me to leave in the evening for interviews and meetings. We required babysitters if we both needed to go and even when Beth was on call and I went out by myself. This became more difficult as our family grew to four children.

Though we did not achieve our great financial goal through it, yet because it taught me business principles, I count the experience to be a positive one. Setbacks and moves required us to start and stop a few times. Others might have overcome their obstacles. We just didn't.

All throughout this time I kept up with the piano while also writing songs. Playing the piano lifted my spirits when I needed them lifted and soothed my anxiety and restlessness when those needed calming. Some interesting melodies emerged. The classes in music theory back in high school now became an important element of my musical growth. I also felt it important for the kids to hear music coming from an instrument, not only from television, radio, or recordings. Because music played a big part of my life, I believe it did something subconsciously that would always ground them in some solid way.

The rocking chair mellowed the mood in the same way. My mother maintained that rocking a baby in a rocking chair is good for both the baby and the person holding the baby. Rocking the babies to sleep at night calmed me too, almost always. Most nights went easily. I loved to rock them to sleep, to gently run my fingertips along their temple and over their ear, imagining that many years from then, their one true love would run their fingers in the same way and instantly my kids would understand that person to be the one meant for them. Who knows? It could happen that way. It's just a happy little dream. Watching them sleep gave me such a great sense of satisfaction. There is nothing like the peace that envelopes the house when all the children are home and asleep.

As each got a little older, I would read to them. At times I was so tired, I would be reading with my eyes shut and having no idea what I was saying, nodding off the whole time. Words came out making no sense and certainly not what the page had printed on it. And now that they could read along, they'd poke me and look at me funny saying, "Hey, Dad, that's not what the book says!"

No matter, I'd just start at the top of the page and try to get through it one more time. I believe all children should be surrounded by books and be read to.

One of my favorite sayings that I impart to my children is "The difference between who you are today and who you will be in a year from now is because of the books you read and the people you meet." All of my children are great readers. We encourage it, as both of Beth parents had with her and mine had with me. As a family, we love books.

Spiritual Growth

This may sound as though I'm supposed to say this because it's the right thing to say, but it is true. Of all of the books we have, the one that has influenced me the most is the Bible. Growing up Lutheran and a Christian did not really teach me what it meant to be one or the true depth of it. That came later as did my reliance on the Bible's contents. My two best friends were Jewish, and I spent a lot of time with them and their families. I celebrated the Jewish holidays along with them as my friends would celebrate the Christian holidays with me. Once I reached my teen years, I did not attend church regularly at all. This changed years later when Beth and I were invited to attend a local church. With only a fundamental knowledge of some prayers, some of the proverbs, and some of the scripture from my early Sunday school experiences, it was only now that I read and listened, developing understanding for the first time really what it meant to say I was a Christian. Although I tried to be "good" and live a respectful life, there had to be something more, something I wanted but did not have and discovered that I could find "a peace that goes beyond all understanding." At times, I feel as though I have found that space, while other times, the struggle and the discord of life loom large. And I believe this keeps me searching for truth. Finding this peace is one thing; keeping it is the elusive part. It is a continual quest. Instead of discovering it all at once, it feels like it is meted out in enough portions to satisfy but then to leave me desiring more. I realized my shortcomings and transgressions numbered too many to honestly profess living a good and righteous life. We all have been hurt and have inflicted pain without the intention of doing so. For it all, intentionally or unintentionally, I've needed to forgive and be forgiven. I found out how in the Bible.

My journey has led me in many different directions, always searching for something stable along the way. Through the Word of God and the life, the death, and the resurrection of Jesus, I found a peace that I had not known before.

I will not convince you on what to believe. You will come to your own conclusion. It is not my intention to make you see things the way I see them. That is nearly impossible. What I can tell you is that, from my research, all of the books I have read, and the lectures I have heard, the conclusion I am left with is that Jesus could not have been anyone other than Whom He said He was and that He lived and died as has been told and then rose again on Easter morning. He is beside me always, and when I need Him now, just as in some very difficult periods in my life, I feel His presence and guidance.

It is interesting that certain events happen in a particular order. When we were invited to attend this church, we had not been attending for too long when Beth and I faced one of the most difficult times of our lives. Beth was now almost halfway through another pregnancy when she went in for a checkup. I stood watching during the fetal monitoring, when our doctor determined there was no pulse from the baby. We were in shock. This seemed like a bolt out of the blue. There was nothing to be done that evening, and we drove home with the directions to return the next morning for the delivery. I will never forget the stunned silence of our drive home. The drive, though only twenty miles, seemed like an eternity, and the road appeared abandoned, like we were the only ones on it. Even upon arrival home, there were no real words to say. Once home, we hugged each other and thought it best to inform our parents and a few friends. We went to bed that night in anguished disbelief. Heartache and grief are emotions so deeply personal that words are inadequate describing the experiencing of them.

Our baby, only twenty-one weeks along in the pregnancy, was delivered with her umbilical cord twisted around her tiny body and neck. Her hands and feet, arms, and legs were perfectly formed, with her face resembling a combination of both of her brothers. We could see this all as I held her. We named her Jennifer. Jennifer, from head to toe, was barely longer than the length of my hand, from the tip of my finger to the bottom of my palm.

It was determined that the umbilical cord entanglement was the reason for her demise, and no autopsy was performed.

As exhilarated as we were at the birth of our two boys, we now walked with heavy hearts. The pastor from our church, Dr. Alan Stanford; his wife, Elaine; and a few of our friends came by to console us once we returned home. Jennifer would have been twenty years old as I write this.

Just prior to this time, a fellow at the church would come up to me and say something that I took as a kind of a jab. It was nothing spiteful, mind you, just a verbal dig. I tried to laugh it off and give a good-natured chuckle, not letting him know that they were starting to irritate me. This went on a couple of weeks, and I thought about it quite a bit. Then I had a revelation. He did not really know me, and I did not really know him except for seeing him in church. For him to go out of his way to say something to me over a course of time, I surmised it could have been one of two things: 1.) He just wanted to annoy me for some reason or 2.) this was his way of trying to get to know me. I figured it was the second because in my experience, no one would waste their time just trying to tick someone off for no reason. So the next time he came to launch a verbal dart, I would engage him in a conversation. I called that correctly. We became and still are the best of friends, as are our wives. One of the largest blizzards ever to hit the D.C. area swept through only a couple of weeks after meeting Gary and Jo. Most things were shut down because of this January snowstorm when Gary Hayden called shortly after I had begun to shovel out a luge run down the hill in my backyard for the boys to sled down. I asked him to come over with his family (his wife, Jo, and their three children), and they did. Gary helped me shovel and erect this long twisting run which we later hosed down forming a thin layer of ice to harden it and give it speed. He set up his little hibachi grill, and we grilled burgers on the snow-covered deck. After dressing the kids for the cold and putting on their bike helmets, they were ready for the action of the newly designed snow track that we had toiled over. Lights were set up and lined the way for night sledding. The kids slept well that night. Since we had the lights shining on the run, I went out for a couple of quick runs once the kids and Beth were tucked in. Those couple of runs turned into a couple of hours because each time I got back up to the top, I couldn't resist going down "just one more time." Other than when performing, I felt like a kid again with no worries—just fun! I slept well that night too.

It would be only days later that we would be in the hospital for Jennifer. The lightness and joy of those snow-filled days would now be replaced with a somber sadness.

We had found comfort in friends from church. The church gave us a place to heal. Once we became involved with the church, I found my way back to acting with the drama worship team. The team would produce a skit that would coincide with the pastor's sermon, to give context to the subject. We adapted scripts to fit our message, wrote some original skits, and had a great time performing. It was fun to work with some very talented people. We had found a church home. Gary and Jo became our small group leaders, setting our friendship forever.

No More Illusions

Plantar fasciitis is a condition that is a typical malady for dancers and athletes affecting the arch muscles on the bottom of the feet. The symptoms produce sharp pain that start in the arches, between the heel and the balls of the feet. The pain can shoot up through the calf muscles. Typically, this occurs after being at rest or being in one position and not moving for a period of time. Then when called upon to walk, run, dance, or move, the muscles spasm causing acute and tremendous pain, making it almost impossible to move. This condition is brought on usually by overworking those muscles over time and can be remedied by icing, massage, and therapy. When that does not achieve the desired results, another option is surgery. This was the case for me. After suffering from plantar fasciitis for a considerable length of time with no long-term results from the therapy, I had my left foot operated on. The procedure involved the severing of all of the plantar fascia muscles in the lower arch of the foot and then reattaching half of them. At the same time I had a ruptured bursa in my heel removed. That is the small cushion in the heel of the foot. It is a last resort type of operation for this condition.

Strength in my left foot would be severely compromised. Afterward I could no longer point or curl my toes the way I used to, put my weight on the balls of my feet, and be able to hold that position. My calf muscle would be affected, and I would only hope I could walk without a limp.

I do not walk with a limp, but this surgery ended the possibility of performing mime to the level I required for many years to come. The full strength never fully came back, but I can do most things again, just not as long and not as well when it comes to movement involving my left foot. Turning forty was not a big issue for me. Turning forty-two and having this operation designated finality to my youthful days, to my mime performances. Physically, this setback restricted mobility, but the mental aspect turned out to be more difficult to come to terms with. Life for me has always been about adjustments.

We had lost a baby in the beginning of the year, and the ache that we felt might not have been evident to the outside world after a while but lingered not far below our skin. It did no good to dwell on something that could not be changed. Now my surgery represented a different loss. I fought the battle to remain positive. Inside I was crying. The joy my boys and wife provided kept me from going too deep into any kind of pity. Time did not allow for extended mourning. This part of my journey felt so unkind. Life did not stop for any of this. All the chores and work that needed to get done did not just go away. So I worked through it, as we must do. My boys needed me, and my wife needed me. What would come next? I did not know. But it had to get better. At least I hoped it would get better. Because if it could get worse, that terrible thought does bleed into mind now and then and must be ousted sooner than later.

Beth and I bought a grand piano that fall from my old boss. He knew I had wanted one at some point, and he found one he thought would be great. It was a twenty-year-old used K. Kawai 6′1″ C3. Any piano more than six feet is considered a grand piano. Less than that is a baby grand. I still had the Kohler and Campbell upright piano that I grew up playing, but it could not compare to the sound of the C3. The length of the strings along with the sheer size of the piano, when played, resonated in the house filling it with harmonies and overtones that did not occur in the smaller upright. The touch of the longer keys responded in a way the Kohler and Campbell piano did not. And the sounding board vibrated with reverberating sound making playing the grand a joyful experience.

Les Miserable, the Broadway musical, happened to be on tour appearing in Washington, D.C. that fall. One of the most remarkable musicals in the history of theater required me to have this on my "must see" list, so I bought tickets and we went. Astounding and inspiring only begin to describe what I think to be as perfect a piece of art as there could have ever been created. Something about the pain and agony, the overcoming, and the hope for a better life just touched me so deeply.

At once, I started writing my own music on my new piano. I had been writing a few songs here and there anyway, but after seeing *Les Miserable*, I created more than thirty songs in the next few months. Whatever mood I happened to be in likely ended up as a tune. Much of the time I composed when the boys were taking their nap and over the next year or so penned over a hundred songs, many very good ones and some that, with some more attention, could be made into something. And then many ended up more like an exercise in composition. But this gave me hope, had me dreaming of the future again, and served as therapy, of sorts, relieving the sadness the year had brought.

Between the cooking, the cleaning, the toilet training, the driving and shopping, the activities at church, business meetings, the doctor's appointments, and recovering from a great loss and then a foot surgery, I squeezed in the time to write music hoping it might be a possible road in the future.

Do You Do Parties?

Admitting to being a mime on occasion would many times lead to that question. I almost always said yes, in the beginning, because I could make some money for a few hours of commitment. The gigs were not beneficial to the artistic craft, and after establishing my way on the college circuit, I tried to avoid them. But I would perform more as a favor than a need to. Although younger audiences could be hilarious to perform for, the audience that a kid's party provided could not be classified as my target group. The shows would touch on mime but revolve more on the clowning side of the spectrum, with juggling and magic tricks. I remember it being a constant battle to bridge the conflict between me being treated like an artist or being used as a novelty act. This formed a level of angst in me. Not so much that I did not want to entertain children, I enjoyed that most of the time, but I worked hard to be recognized as a fine artist for all of those years. Twelve years before, I had turned down an opportunity to develop a children's daily television show in South Alabama. One hundred dollars a week and no budget for the show did not entice me in the least. At that time I did not see where that would lead to anything but hard work and little to show for it. It would not pay the bills, and entertaining children in this way would change my direction and focus. Maybe it could have grown to something, but then again maybe not. Here is one choice that might be regarded a missed opportunity, on the surface maybe so, but in the long run, just another fork in the road.

Taking on many odd and silly things along the way, sometimes my mime show didn't fit the bill, and doing a favor for a neighbor helped even if costume characters didn't broaden my repertoire. Sometimes parents talked me into being something else, like the time money ($50.00) induced me to be a Teenage Mutant Ninja Turtle for the neighbor's little boy's birthday party, in a pathetic excuse for a rental costume on its last legs, falling to pieces as I wore it. $150 saw me playing Uncle Sam at a convention casino night on another occasion, or standing on the street corner holding a sign for an opening of a gas station earned me $200. Those were some of the longest hours of my life. I always gave my all, but sometimes a show didn't pop. Torture comes in many disguises.

When performing for birthday parties, smaller children routinely gravitated closer and slowly encroached my makeshift stage until they virtually surrounded my feet. It is just in their nature. To combat this (and it sometimes felt like combat), I hid a big bag of candy, placed upstage, out of sight; so when they edged up, I'd run back to the candy, grab a handful, and throw it over their heads. They chased the candy gathering it all up. When they turned around again with their treats, I would be standing straight up with my palm held out in the stop position. They would stop and sit down. As the show continued, they gradually began the same migration toward me. I repeated the process making it part of the act.

But I must say, of all the costumed events that I performed, the most humiliating had to be at my own son's fifth birthday party. This celebration was a really wonderful concept on paper. I really could not perform just yet because of the foot surgery, so performing for my own child's birthday would be tough gig anyway. Instead, we rented the movie theater for a private showing of the rereleased *Star Wars* one Saturday morning, inviting Jamie's entire class and parents and friends to the special showing. Each received soda and a bag of popcorn. After the show we all were to continue the party at our church in the community room with everything decorated *Star Wars*. We served sandwiches and ice cream and cake, and to add to the delight of the children, we handed out light sabers. What a really cool party. Considering all we did, it didn't cost a fortune. But, while the movie played, kept secret from me, my wife picked up a Darth Vader costume for me to wear adding the crowning glory to this festive occasion. At the time it seemed like a pretty awesome idea. My transformation into Darth Vader took place in one of the men's bathrooms including my imitating the voice that James Earl Jones made so famous, saying, "Luke, you are my son!" as it reverberated in my ears quite majestically inside the authentic black helmet. I geared up for this magnificent appearance while concurrently the kids were being given their light sabers. Now, with the coordination of the *Star Wars* music filling the hall and with the cue from my wife, I gallantly entered one end of the hall. What a spectacular entrance! With long gallant strides down the long corridor, anticipation built as the enormous presence of the Dark Side swept in, with the long black cape trailing splendidly behind.

I could not have glided in more than a dozen steps when the shrieks of joy, the chaos, and tumult that I could see through the slit of the helmet erupted. Within seconds the pummeling of Darth Vader by twenty-five little five-year-olds (and my guess a couple of adults) with their newly acquired light sabers commenced. Immediately I decided that the meet and greet and book signing I had envisioned would now be ill-advised, not breaking stride and continuing straight out the door (inconveniently placed at the far end of the hall) while being slashed, pummeled, and brutalized by this new class of Jedi knights. For some reason this upset me. When changing back into my clothes in a men's room far, far away, my son and one of his friends followed, and because of the costume I did not see them do so. They trailed me and snuck up behind and then flew the door open just as I removed my helmet, catching Darth Vader transforming back into Dad. I snarled at them to "Get out of here!" They looked stunned and then laughed as they ran down the hall cackling as if discovering the evil Santa Claus. Well, with the secret out, I reappeared as Dad to the little superheroes' shrieks, mocking me and screaming, "Look! It's Darth Vader! You were Darth Vader." Then they started hitting me again with their sabers. The parents were crying with laughter as they took their Jedi kids off of me. So much for illusions of grandeur! I still contend there were adults wielding the light sabers too.

Maybe this fiasco made this a more memorable party for my son and those who attended. It took little time for me to soothe my bruised ego to laugh at the whole episode as extremely funny. I did learn two things for sure: Do not give out the party favors until the party is over, and avoid being the villain without reinforcements.

Sleeping at odd times became a way of life. Getting a full night's sleep without interruption would be a near impossibility now. Walking around tired remained the status quo. Grocery shopping with two little ones kept the mind occupied even though it was draining. On one occasion during a typical grocery shopping trip, the boys and I filled the cart quite high and made it through the checkout with no major hassles. Proceeding to the car, I loaded them and buckled them up in their car seats. They quickly fell asleep on the way home, a good ten miles away. After pulling into the driveway and gingerly carrying them both up to their beds one at a time while they continued to sleep, I sat down to catch my breath for a moment following this cardio workout from all of the stairs traversed. The two little angels slept, and a wonderful peace came over me. After thirty seconds or so, I quietly stood up and tiptoed out of the room and headed back down to the car to bring the groceries in. Going to the back hatch of the van, I discovered there were no groceries in the car which surprised me until the "Oh crap!" moment hit me between the eyes. The cart loaded with bags was left abandoned at the curb outside of the grocery store! My boys were loaded but not the groceries! In a desperate phone call to the store, the manager calmed my panicked voice and told me he had wheeled the cart to the back of the store and into the huge freezer unit. He laughed saying they were taking bets on how long it would take for someone to notice the missing food. Well, now I had to carry the boys back down, put them in their car seats one at a time, and drive back to the store to retrieve the food. I got to the store, unloaded the boys, went in and got the cart, went back to the car, loaded the boys into the car, and this time remembered the groceries, now having to drive home again as the kids resumed their naps on the way. This time waking them up when we got back, I plugged in a movie for them to watch, gave them their juice cups, unloaded and put the groceries away, and once done sat between them as they watched their movie. I closed my eyes for a few minutes until the phone rang interrupting a very short nap just in time to walk the dogs and then make dinner.

Joshua: Christmas Came Early

With only two to watch over, finding the culprit could not be much easier. After two, it became a blur. That blur came in the package named Joshua. Born only five days before Christmas, this little guy arrived with no complications. Beth's pregnancy went very smoothly. In the back of our minds, during the pregnancy the uneasiness lingered until around the thirty-two-week mark, but we did not talk those concerns. With each delivery, I took a more active part in the birthing experience. The birth of Joshua made me appreciate the absolute miracle that birth is. All of the things that could go so right and all the things that could go so wrong were now part

179

of the overall understanding that I did not fully recognize prior to this. Entering our world and taking his first breath bore much more weight as Joshua established his position in our family.

What an enormous relief.

Within minutes of bringing Joshua home, we posed Jamie and Jeremy holding him for a few quick pictures. I made sure all were settled in, the kids, Beth, and her parents, and then ran out with the film to get it developed to have prints made at a one-hour photo shop. I had addressed the Christmas card envelopes a few days earlier and, when I returned, slipped a picture of the three boys into the cards, sealed the envelopes, and went to the post office, only a mile away, to mail them. This was December 22. Most of them were delivered by the 24th. It may not sound like a big deal, yet it has been a source of pride that I got that done so quickly, and our friends were surprised at the speed of this news. Of course now we have the internet, and this does not sound like such a big deal. If all things could work so smoothly!

Joshua arrived on December 20. Coincidentally five years before, we had conceived Jeremy. On the one hand, it is great that we could pinpoint the date. On the other hand, it gives you a little insight because we actually could pinpoint the exact day. Still, the fact that we conceived one and delivered another five years apart on the same date makes a unique little story.

We now graduated to the family van era and traded our lovely sedan in to accommodate the burgeoning family. Speaking of burgeoning, on the wrapper of the diapers, it is mentioned that they are good for up to twenty-two pounds. I can tell you they do not come close to holding that much. See for yourself, but it is here that it might be wise to learn from someone else's experience.

Having three children requiring different activities and toys, books, and friends now changed the dynamics around the house. The stresses of the different parts of the day expanded with the needs of a third little one. The amount of different-sized traveling equipment created a small nightmare in itself. Double strollers, portable cribs, and car seats only begin to fill the list of necessities. Juggling classes did not cover this, and if they did, I must have missed them.

By this time, the older ones could do their own walking, a rare saving grace, but created a whole new set of concerns.

Going out into the world with three kids in tow and only two hands presented me with problems too. Without dwelling on the subject, let me just say all public bathrooms are not created equal. Facilities with baby diaper changing accommodations in men's rooms are now commonplace, not like twenty-five years ago. Society has recognized that many men now share these tasks.

In those early days of fatherhood, I tried to shield the boys from the real world to some extent. We did not let them watch certain types of television shows. Anything that had some real element of violence in it we worked hard at protecting them from, not allowing them to use any kind of gun toys. That didn't last too long though. Jamie would take Popsicle sticks, bend them in half, and go "Bang! Bang!" Where did he learn that? I do not know. We would be going through the grocery store, and he would ask every man he encountered, "Hi, what's your name? Do you have a gun?"

"Oh, now isn't that cute?" we would add.

We had Jamie modify it to "What kind of car do you have?"

Once we realized that forbidding everything supposedly offensive and overseeing every moment would never be sustainable until they graduated college. We gave up that overcontrolling practice.

This is the story that drove that point home.

Electric power in our neighborhood got knocked out by a raging snowstorm. When this happened, it couldn't be determined if there would be no power for a day or three. It's usually no more than that but still a hassle to deal with. We could exist without electricity in the short term, but we needed electricity to power the water pump at the bottom of our well. No electricity prevented the flow of water to the house. For this reason we checked into a local hotel for a couple of days where power had not been affected. On this occasion, Beth and the boys made it up to the room as I followed with a load of luggage. Five-year-old Jamie and four-year-old Jeremy found their way to the end of the bed, sitting directly in front of the television, watching with rapt attention as I put the luggage down and joined them watching *Xena: The Princess Warrior*, a television show they had never seen because we had monitored their viewing up to this point. This was a new experience for both boys. For those who do not know who Xena is, she is a stunningly beautiful defender of good.

In this episode, she swung down from the branches of a tree, surprising a half-dozen villains, kicking, flipping, and beating them up until they were all disabled or had run off. As they were strewn across the ground around the feet of the buxom beauty, Xena stood firmly with her fists on her hips surveying her vanquished foes with great pride.

It was at that very moment that Jamie, my wide-eyed, awestruck, slack-jawed little boy, exclaimed in total astonishment, "Wow! That's my kind of woman!"

As parents, we elect positions that we think are solid and important. Sometimes, though, we need to reevaluate them from time to time. In thinking we were protecting our kids from unwanted influences, it dawned on us that this policy in our home merely made us feel like we were being good parents. Sure, it was a good idea to monitor their viewing intake, but excessive control proved fruitless in the long run. Relaxing the grip on the television remote also allowed for teaching moments when we thought there might be something that went overboard.

Raising my boys had me reading all sorts of books on the subject of raising children. It is my experience now that we, as parents, have only a range of influence. Other factors come into play in determining our children's future as well. Family structure or birth order is one area that plays a part. The research on this predicts many traits that I have found to be accurate. Coming from a family of six children has given me my own observations when matched to the research. Identifying the way we interact with each also helped to see patterns that fit the relationships. I could see character traits each sibling displayed precisely detailed according to the studies.

Forgive the repetition, but parenting, whether the mother or father stays at home or otherwise, is left in the hands of people on a huge learning curve that does not stop. Each stage of development is a new area of study. Each additional child changes the equation. There is no set formula that you can count on, only probabilities.

And those always have exceptions to the rules. What worked well for the first child may not ever conform to the second or third or subsequent children's needs. And I will tell you here that as they mature, the grid is expanded and the options are complex. A simple yes or no has to be weighed with consideration for future ramifications, not just the immediate situation, or even past rules might be in jeopardy of having to be modified to accommodate the new circumstances. Imagine dancing on an undulating chessboard and having to stay only on the white squares or the black squares but not both. That's what this feels like sometimes. Even with a good set of foundational principles to guide, there is always an exception waiting to pressure your reconsideration.

Look at a coach in a football game, for example. He goes in with a book of plays to choose from. The players will try to work within that framework, but there will always be those broken plays that have to be accounted for. Having the playbook keeps order; and when confronted with having to adapt, the team will, hopefully, not descend into chaos. There is a guide they can reference to get back on course. So it is with being a family. This goes back to my analogy of being a fine marksman needing to have a frame of reference.

Jamie spent his kindergarten year in public school. We watched him ascend the school bus stairs the first time on Jeremy's fourth birthday. After seeing the bus disappear down the road, a pregnant Beth, Jeremy, and I headed back up the gravel driveway as I videotaped the event. Now having the full spotlight, Jeremy ran up to the camera and, with me recording, spun around once while looking at the lens and asked, "Did you see my twist?" He then started up the driveway and proceeded to slip and cut his knee on the stones. The swings of emotion can happen quickly and are typical in the everyday life of a family. Nothing stays calm and stable for long. There are always transitions and adaptations to reckon with.

The following year, when Jeremy began school and Jamie graduated to first grade, we enrolled them in a newly established private Christian school at our church. Responsibility for transportation fell to the parents and thus began my ritual of driving our little prodigies to and from school every day. Over the next twenty years, this became the routine and now part of my job description. Being a stay-at-home dad afforded me the time to do this. The car provided a space to teach along the way. I had a captive audience. I tried to touch on many subjects and in many areas. Serious or humorous, it didn't matter. I imparted my vast wealth of "wisdom" incrementally to them during these round-trips. As to whether they learned anything or not, you'll have to ask them. I am sure some of it stuck, even if this now triggers an "Oh no, here comes another lecture!" response every time I open my mouth to say something to them.

My quest for teaching might not have matched their quest for learning, but I tried to keep up nonetheless.

What child does not love watermelon? And with the watermelon come the seeds. With the seeds come the questions.

"Why are there seeds in watermelons?" one of the boys would ask.

"Seeds are for making more watermelons," I would say.

"How?"

"By planting them in a garden and then watering them, then watermelons come. They grow from the tiny seeds to great big watermelons," I said hoping this would satisfy them. It didn't.

"Can we plant the seeds and grow watermelons?"

"Sure."

"Now?" Jeremy asked.

"Sure."

So we took the seeds and planted them out in a little makeshift garden and watered the seeds. We watered those seeds every day. A week went by, and there was nothing. Two weeks went by, and there was still nothing. It was obvious to me that not even one seed germinated, but I would not tell the boys that. We just kept watering for another week or so. I snuck out and bought a few watermelons without them knowing, "planting" them out in the garden, so when it came time for the boys to water the garden, the surprise crop overwhelmed them with joy at the magnificence of nature in providing, overnight, glorious watermelon bounty.

They were astounded and giddy upon the watermelon discovery as they danced around, jumping up and down, thrilled to be farmers, with Daddy elevated, once again, in their eyes. I'm sure glad I took off the little store stickers.

Becoming a Deacon and a Gideon

Underneath all of this, there comes into play our own core values and principles on which we stand. We all have them, and many are firmly set. Adhering to them in every condition is almost impossible, even with the very best intentions. The chance that we fall short within our own boundaries gives a little insight to how children will push against theirs. The fact is we are only guides. We can teach all we want, but if they do not want to hear it, they will find out from their own mistakes. Keeping them alive becomes the challenge, hoping they will live long enough to see how brilliant of parents we are.

And though our young ones may not respect our rules, the universe has rules that are immutable. I know them as God's laws. They are unassailable, absolute, and irrefutable. We taught our children this. They may not choose to believe it, or they may sway from it, but they are taught this in my house. Again, it's not my place to demand compliance to this philosophy. This will have to be discovered fully on the paths they travel to these truths. Discerning this on my journey through life happened far into my adult life, so how can I expect that I can impart my own realizations emphatically and permanently onto someone else? That is not in my job description. Any convincing in this realm must be done with the gathering of enough evidence until the facts satisfy the seeker's conclusion.

My church elected me to the position of deacon, an honor I hold as dearly as my degree from college. I attained here, among the men of the church, that measure of confidence that always seemed to be missing in my life. Let's face it. I had not attained the level of fame and fortune to this point that I had set out to do in my professional career, and having held many jobs along the way gave me no sense of permanence or standing. Though having been elected to and holding a number of leadership positions you might think would give some stature, the fact is a stay-at-home father (or mother, for that matter), although extremely important, attracts little accolades from modern-day society; and that remains an injustice, to my mind. A high level of prestige is not bestowed upon a full time parent, regardless of the importance of the position, and to be a male in a traditionally female role quite apparently downgraded my status in the eyes of other men. Or so it seemed to be the prevailing societal wave of opinion. These perceptions, of course, had their exceptions.

Having progressed to include a diverse past, a college education, and numerous successes countered any attempt to pigeonhole me and designate me insignificant. In truth, I am sure many men would have loved to do what I do. And their opinion, quite frankly, would not have convinced me to forsake my new job description anyway. No doubt this unconventional life choice knocks up against standard family blueprints. That does not mean there were no times of being a little self-conscious about it all.

The men who have the opportunity to stay home to raise their children should be applauded and celebrated. The denigration of a stay-at-home parent has been slowly mitigated somewhat over the past twenty-five years with more families seeing the value it provides the children of such an upbringing. Of course, women have been fighting this battle for a whole lot longer. My mother, for example, when asked what she did, would answer with a very humble "I'm just a mom." That has been the attitude that has been projected onto a stay-at-home parent for decades, as if one of the most important and difficult jobs in the world, the raising of our children, is a throwaway life.

Couples are not always afforded the choice of having a parent stay home with their children. I am in no way implying that is wrong. We all have to do what suits our needs. This is a very individualized arrangement based on the family's goals and circumstances. It seems we are scrutinized no matter what the decision happens to be. If you are seeking approval from the outside world, you may find that the opinions will vary anyway, so it is best to find comfort in your own position to your own course of action.

Coming in from a position of not holding an occupation well regarded in social circles, my appointment to deacon came with the side benefit of acceptance, this time not by what I did but whom I was. From the time I was a freshman in high school and elected president of the class to now becoming a deacon, I had not reflected on the whole body of work I had accomplished. All seemed fragmented and disjointed up until this moment.

A few of my fellow deacons were also members of the Gideons, an organization that is well known for distributing Bibles and other good works. I was invited to join and did so. We would visit jails and hospitals, place Bibles in hotels, and talk with people about the Word of God. When I traveled throughout my career, I frequently read the Bible that was in my motel or hotel room, never thinking that one day I would get the chance to distribute them.

My path had not been ordinary, as you can see. Somehow I had allowed, at moments, my subconscious to find fault in the choice of being a stay-at-home dad in assuming an apologetic undertone when asked my profession. Even now, when filling out applications, writing in househusband, stay at home father, or homemaker on the occupation line is extremely difficult. Although there is nothing in the world to be ashamed of, there still is that battle with my ego which wishes to jot down something with seemingly more power and significance.

No matter that my wife and I are in a partnership where the delineation of duties happens to cross traditional lines, it still takes a conscious effort each time to justify this. It just goes to show you how entrenched the norms are in our psyche. To break away from those norms takes an unspoken courage to go against the grain, in this example of *Mr. Mom* or any other.

Aren't we all more than our job description? But that is what we do. We box in our opinions of people very quickly with only bits of information about them.

Once in a while, I have had interactions that went something like this. If not precisely these words, most certainly they were implied. Or maybe adjusting to my own insecurity about being a stay-at-home father painted these conversations:

"Briefly tell me everything I need to know about yourself in seven seconds. You're a what? A mime? What's that? You're a what? A stay-at-home dad? You're kidding me? You're a what? An actor? Now you are kidding me. What movies have you done? None? See you're no actor. What else did you say you did? You write music? Sure you do. Come on. Tell me something that I can believe. You're a deacon in the church? Oh, come on now. You're killing me. Alright then, let's get serious here. What does your wife do? She's a surgeon? You just don't stop, do you? She really is a doctor? How'd she end up with you? What did you say you did again? Oh, that's right. You don't work."

There is no question there were times I placed the inferior label on myself. But then I had to quickly shake off those momentary questionings. Momentary is the word because to linger in that space gave more power to it. Realizing this was my path and knowing what was right for me but might not be right for everyone else ended the fleeting self-doubt. There were times it might have been wished to have a simple job description for expediency or even acceptance, to soothe or protect my ego somewhat; but in truth, knowing that I provided for my family what no one else in the world could didn't need a defense. The little internal battle going on with myself always bowed to that fact by knowing my value to those who mattered. But yes, from time to time those feelings crept in.

Each year the estimated pay a full time parent would be compensated, based on the different types of duties they typically perform in the rearing of the children, the keeping of the house, and other factors, is calculated. As I write, this year's number exceeds $65,000.00 per year. I wonder if this includes overtime or on-call compensation. Nevertheless, this is significant amount and would be considered a fine salary in today's world not drawing criticism in too many circles. Some families determine it is feasible to have both partners working. Different conditions require different approaches. We considered the cost of daycare, commute and travel costs, meal and snack costs while on the job, wardrobe expenses, and additional income tax outlay to determine how much it would require in salary to justify working a full-time job. It made no sense to us for both to be absent from running the house and raising the children, where our previously determined priorities rested, to realize a moderately insignificant bump in actualized income that could achieved alternately by working some plan from the home. Marriage and parenthood redirect many of our individual propensities by guiding us away from self to include the care of others. A balance must be found so self is not completely swallowed up in a false sense of martyrdom. After all, isn't it our purpose to grow in all directions and not thwart or stifle the things or others we have determined need our utmost attention?

In September, a few months before Joshua would be born and a month past the twenty-one-week mark of Beth's pregnancy, the gestation point we discovered the baby's fetal demise more than a year and a half ago, we started to relax a bit in anticipation of a new child. A baby born at this stage would be viable, notwithstanding complications. The memory of that never leaves. We have a friend who, at almost thirty-nine weeks along in her pregnancy, suffered a placental abruption, where the placenta peels away, partially or com-pletely from the inner wall of the uterus, depriving the baby food and oxygen. Urgent and immediate attention to save the baby could not be attained, with a hospital too far away to emergently deliver her child. She also, like Beth, had to drive home with the knowledge of carrying a stillborn baby. There is no doubt in my mind that this kind of tragedy has a profound effect on couples, women in partic-ular. She and her husband's faith in God carried them through that time, and because of their example, we also found strength in our sorrowful times. Words may never be uttered, but underneath there is a deep sense of loss that never heals over. Yet we all are affected. Some show it more; some hide it more than others.

Another example of a mother's grief occurred in an unexpected scenario. Our dog had given birth to six puppies. The last of them, the runt of the litter, struggled for a time. We had placed a little rag doll in with all of the puppies. Cinnamon, our new mother, attended them all, paying special attention to the little one. He did not make it past one day. The joy diminished by this loss. Cinnamon carried the little rag doll around in her teeth, like she would a pup, by the scruff of its neck, for weeks. At one point, soon after the puppy died, she retreated to a favorite spot under our bed and proceeded to rip and tear up the underside of the box spring. So grief is real, and it needs to be expressed and acknowledged.

In speaking of death, it reminds us that the gift is in life itself and even the little things we do add to the tapestry of our own making.

Déjà Vu

In the spring of 1998, Beth found me extremely attractive and quite irresistible for that short window of time each month in which ovulation commands respect and attention. Somehow she ended up pregnant again. Since having three boys, life blurred anyway. One more only added to the happiness. This would put the age of Joshua and the new baby about two years apart. Sometime near the beginning of June, we learned it would be a baby girl. Of course, we welcomed this wonderful news.

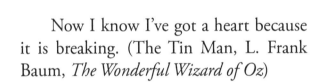

Now I know I've got a heart because it is breaking. (The Tin Man, L. Frank Baum, *The Wonderful Wizard of Oz*)

Anguish

In the middle of August, we went to Beth's routine checkup at her OB-GYN doctor's office. Unbelievably, the sonogram could not detect a heartbeat from the fetus. Again, we sat in stunned silence. Could this be repeating? Once more, we drove back home only to have to return to the hospital for the delivery. We had to make arrangements for the boys and their care while we went to the hospital. None of this seemed real. Could this really be déjà vu? How could this be happening again? That's the question that kept ringing through both of our heads. The doctor induced labor to deliver the baby, as had been before, with Sarah being born in the same manner as our lost Jennifer. And like Jennifer, she too entangled in her umbilical cord, only this time it wrapped around her legs. She too gestated to twenty weeks or so. She too had perfect little hands and feet with all of her fingers and toes. She too was perfectly formed in every way, as we could even see her facial features taking on, as Jennifer's did, the resemblance of her brothers'. As I gently cradled our stillborn Sarah in the palm of my hand in the same fashion as I did Jennifer, again, tears could not wash away the ache we were experiencing. For this to happen to us once more resurrected and compounded our pain. We were devastated, numb, and confounded.

The cause of the baby's demise, again, believed to be the result of the umbilical cord wrapping around Sarah. This time, however, we sent her off for an autopsy to be performed, unlike Jennifer. The report came back that Sarah had expired from the lack of nutrition and that the umbilical cord entanglement was the result of the struggle to be fed and not the cause of the demise. Antiphospholipid antibody syndrome (APS) is an autoimmune disorder that, during pregnancy, increases risk of fetal demise. In layman's terms, this caused an imbalance in the amniotic fluid that created an autoimmune type of response between Beth and the baby.

Once determined by a specialist at Georgetown University Hospital, he said this could be neutralized by having Beth take an aspirin every day. How simple a solution this seemed we thought. This, of course, had us second-guessing the decision we made not to have an autopsy on Jennifer. We were convinced that explanation could also be applied to the cause of Jennifer's death. Then we considered Joshua, with his birth weight the least of the boys. Jamie and Jeremy were both 6 lbs. and 12 oz. Joshua weighed only 6 lbs. and 4 oz.

The specialist told us that there should be no fear in trying again to have a baby if this remedy were followed. With that assurance we did not try to prevent our attempt to have another baby. Within a few months Beth again found me quite attractive and irresistible, as described earlier, and like magic pregnant again, but this time having taken the aspirin each day. This pregnancy went along smoothly. We kept our fingers crossed and maintained hope in our hearts.

Many times we would be out with the boys, and people seeing that Beth in a "family way" would say, "So you're trying for a little girl?"

"No, that part doesn't really matter to us," we would usually respond. And it didn't.

Beth and I thought it best not to find out beforehand, the sex of the baby. We wanted healthy to be the first consideration. Because Joshua made his entrance as such a gorgeous baby, we did have one more hope: that, if a girl, she be as beautiful a baby as Joshua.

There is a book by Lennart Nilsson and Lars Hamberger called *A Child Is Born* with pictures and commentary on the birth of a child. The pictures are amazing photos of the actual developmental stages of a fetus inside the womb. Jamie now arriving at the grand age of eight years old, as the time got closer for Beth to have the baby, asked, "Why does Mommy have to have the baby?"

This was a perfect opportunity to bring out the book and show him all about the process. Where should I start? Why, at the beginning, of course. So I began.

I told him of the penis and the vagina, the sperm and the egg, and how they got to meet up with each other and told him people called this having sex. And God made it so when people got married, they could have families. Jamie looked down at the pictures, then looked up at me, and asked with a touch of disdain, "When I get married, do I have to have sex?"

I just answered, "You don't need to think about that right now. Marriage itself will answer that question." As I left the room, book in hand, I said, "We'll talk more about this later." I might have jumped the gun on that lesson.

Because of the past events, we decided to go with an OB-GYN who worked closer to us and worked out of the same hospital Beth did. We decided it best to arrange a date close to the due date and induce labor because of our past experiences. A Saturday delivery worked well for the doctor and for us because the hospital would not be as busy and he could give his full attention. He asked me if I would like to deliver the baby. Of course, he said he would be there to give me a few pointers if I needed them. So now I would be in the front row seat for the main event.

Knowing that all progressed well still did not completely erase the trepidation we felt leading up to the birth. The day before we were to go into the hospital, we arranged a photo shoot of the three boys to demark the last day before they had a new sibling, changing the dynamics of the family. This kept our minds busy getting them ready and having a fun time setting up different shots with the same photographer who also photographed our wedding years earlier.

Saturday morning arrived. Off we went to the hospital. Once checked in, we assumed the room with our things; and in short order with the epidural efficiently administered, Beth received the inducement formula while we waited for all things to progress. Not wanting a full graphic record of the event, I had time to set up the camera aiming it from above Beth's right shoulder. Our friend Marie would be there to run the camera. After Beth first delivered Jamie by C-section, all of the rest of the deliveries were vaginal birth after caesarian (VBAC).

Now the time had come for me to scrub and dress in preparation for the birth, the clock showing a few minutes into the afternoon. Jamie had been born at 5:43 p.m., Jeremy at 3:21 p.m., and Joshua at 1:23 p.m. We were thinking this baby would come at 12:34 p.m. We would have to wait five more minutes beyond that prediction before I caught our new baby girl.

The doctor announced, "It's a girl. She has dimples, and she looks just like Mama!"

We named her Jenna. She weighed 8 lbs. and 4 oz., significantly heavier than her brothers at birth. The aspirin a day had indeed made a difference.

Miraculous describes the journey to birth perfectly. Considering all the things that need to transpire, the magnificence of a successful birth is truly awe-inspiring. Knowing we had children waiting for us at home helped us through the sorrowful deliveries, thankful too, because we know there are times when an empty house is all that awaits some who go through that experience.

The comment now when talking about our three boys and their younger sister is "So you kept trying until you got a little girl!"

I would simply and kindly say, "Yes," because the long answer is still difficult to express.

It can be easy to cry out for something that didn't work out as hoped or planned for. I have found it best to be thankful for what has. To dwell on what might have been takes away from what will be and what is. Building a family can have its heartaches along the way. We are blessed to have four healthy children when all is said and done.

"Do not the most moving moments of
our lives find us without words?"

—Marcel Marceau

CHAPTER
10

THE YOUNG FAMILY

In-Laws

From the time of our marriage, Beth's parents, Hermie and Douglas, would come to visit. They lived over two hours away from us. Therefore, they would typically stay for three or four days at a time, sometimes pressing into nearly a week.

Hermie had been diagnosed with diabetes a few years earlier and by the mid-1990s started feeling the ramifications of the disease. As time went on, her eyesight became severely affected from macular degeneration diminishing her sight to the extent that she could only see as one would by looking through a pinhole. Her mobility relegated to walking with a cane and soon to a wheelchair although she could ambulate without it if needed. All the while her kidneys were beginning to shut down, leading her to in-home, nightly kidney dialysis. But her mind remained sharp, being able to recall even the most minute details, down to being able to instruct us in finding a certain length of thread in a particular box or a red button in a remote corner of a dresser drawer in her home or remembering dates, birthdays, and anniversaries. But now these visits would extend for sometimes a week or two at a time and occurred much more frequently.

Douglas, a good bit older than Hermie and while still being physically able, had his own set of issues now affected by the onset of dementia. What were long detailed stories, including those of his participation in World War II, would soon be shortened in length and scope.

They would laugh that Hermie supplied the brains of the outfit and Douglas provided the brawn. Along with taking care of the family, we now cared for my in-laws frequently weeks at a time too. While Beth worked, my staying home made this possible.

Sleep became a luxury with four children, three dogs, two in-laws, and a very busy wife keeping the action moving. I could not keep running down to pick up the folks and driving them back. For safety, we prohibited Douglas to drive anymore, his reactions hampered by his aging. Staying with us could only be a short-term solution to their needs. They could not, reasonably, stay in their home anymore. Although still somewhat able to do things together, they needed and we found an assisted living home between our house and Beth's office. The only stipulations were that they could evacuate the facility without the use of the wheelchair and that Hermie needed to have a shunt put in her arm to switch her over to hemodialysis because it would not be allowed to continue with the nightly dialysis method. We moved much of their furniture in setting up the new apartment. While doing so, Hermie went to sit in a chair and missed it, falling on her coccyx and breaking it, still being admitted to the hospital for the shunt to be put in her arm to accommodate the dialysis treatment hoping that when released she would be well enough to walk. This did not happen. She could not pass the evacuation test at the time because of the earlier fall and pain in her lower back. Rehabilitation for her new ailment now meant that Douglas remained at our house to stay while I moved all of the furniture of theirs to our unfinished basement. When I say I moved the furniture, I must tell you there were friends who helped me do so. It was hard enough to move them once, but to have to do so within the month was an indication of what great friends I had. I might have lost one or two from that experience.

To complicate life even further, Hermie already in rehab for her coccyx started kidney dialysis. The facility for the dialysis next to Beth's office was located fifteen miles down the road from the rehab center on top of the seven more miles from our house. Three days a week, Hermie needed to be in the dialysis chair by 4:30 a.m. and then be picked up at 11:00 a.m. I would pick Hermie up from the rehab center and transport her for her treatment at 4:30 a.m. and go back home. Beth would be getting ready for work after setting up breakfast for the kids and her dad. I would get the kids ready for school and, after they had eaten, drop them off at school and return home to help Douglas with anything he needed and do whatever needed to be done for Joshua and Jenna. Then I would load up the younger ones and go pick up Hermie and return her to the rehab center. This went on for a month before Hermie came back to our house. This streamlined the delivery a bit, but it was a brutally hectic schedule to maintain with all of this now extending through the midst of an unusually cold winter. In a couple of months, we would secure another assisted living home closer to our home, not requiring any stairs to negotiate, moving them in and arranging for round-trip transportation to dialysis.

While moving some of Beth's furniture in her office, I happened upon a mailed brochure advertising an otolaryngology position in Southeast Georgia. Normally, this would just have been tossed away with no regard. The stress of the past few years, having a growing family, losing two babies, taking care of aging parents, covering three offices and working out of two hospitals and a surgery center, running a large home, and looking for some way to simplify our lives, made this brochure jump out at us. The compounding pressure made entertaining a thought of moving quite appealing if we knew it could relieve the stress.

This is the one of the few times, looking back, I wonder how things would have turned out had we not gone. Beth's mother died within the year that we moved. Once we had settled in, we found an assisted living home near us, moving all of Hermie and Douglas's things down. Hermie found her way in and out of the hospital for different reasons a couple of times that spring. On her first admission to the hospital, not even a month after moving, her diet would be restricted; and not wanting to accommodate it caused the new assisted living home to reject the care of Hermie once she got out of the hospital. It forced us to find another assisted living home for Hermie and Douglas and once again move all of their things.

In July she became very loopy and incoherent due to a low oxygenation level in her blood. As with prior hospital visits, we thought she would rebound to again rejoin Douglas. Her passing away came quite unexpectedly, even knowing she wouldn't last many more years. Still, in spite of her fragility, her quick death surprised us.

Over the next two-and-a-half years, Douglas continued the long road of Alzheimer's disease, had his cancerous eye enucleated, and subsequently fell and broke his hip. We were told that having a hip replacement would get him to the point of ambulating with the help of a walker, if all went well, and given reason to believe this to be true. Yet, after the surgery and the stay at the rehabilitation hospital, Douglas's condition worsened. He could not straighten his leg (even with therapy). Now becoming bedridden, his communication ability had digressed. Adding to the burden, insurance coverage was ending.

We converted Jenna's bedroom into a hospital suite and took charge of the care of Beth's father. Josh and Jenna shared a room now. A nurse would come in once a day to check Douglas's vital signs. Other than that, all of the feeding tubes and the monitors that beeped and dinged were our responsibility. Now completely bedridden, we also were in charge of turning him over and cleaning him up, dressing bedsores that developed because of the limited movement, and, generally, nursing him. We did so for his final three months of life. These were some of the most demanding months of our lives. No one cared to give up their dignity even in these circumstances, and we did our very best to make him comfortable while he lay helpless to do anything but submit to his condition. Dying can be an arduous journey. Yet sudden or laborious, when death does come, there is a bewildering sense of shock that is left.

So here again it is just as Marcel Marceau said to me once, "Death—a very strange phenomenon!"

Growing up, my father would say to us on many occasions, "We can only make decisions with the information that we have available to us at the time, and we do the best we can with what we have."

Beth and I did the best we knew how with all that we knew. Our generation is now being called "the Sandwich Generation" because we are not only taking care of our young families. We can also be taking care of our aging parents. As we endured this difficult task, and it certainly couldn't be described as a convenient situation, there were no regrets as to the rightness of it.

What is sometimes lost on us in this scenario is the cost that the children must bear: hours of unwanted car rides, visits, and time away from their friends and home or parents who are too busy or too tired to give them more attention than they do. Then again, that becomes the fabric of their memories. Imaginations are spurred on, and adventures spring from even the most mundane events in a child's eyes. Years from now I may hear the stories where this or that was the starting point of something that became instrumental in why they do a thing a certain way. Having the children participating in activities, sometimes against their desires, and wanting to do another is just the way life is. As parents, we are the guides through their young lives. It may seem that it is the other way around at times and that may be true on occasion, but we are the big people in the room. They will get to choose later on. For now, it is our influence that leads the way. At least we think so, or hope so.

So while there are sacrifices that children must make, there are lessons that go along with that. It teaches them that the world does not revolve around them exclusively. It can be taught that fulfilling an obligation or task may not be exactly our desire at the moment either, yet it is what is right and needs to be done, usually for the benefit of others. The ability to push beyond their selfish nature, even once in a while, when they really wish to focus on their own selves is not an easy lesson to learn. I can attest to that. Don't we all want the convenient and comfortable way that predominantly feeds our own desires? Going outside of that is the opposite—uncomfortable and inconvenient. Stepping away from the selfish and crossing to the selfless will possibly be contrary to the direction we face, leading to adjusting our mind-set to accommodate the new plan to include others. By doing so, we also demonstrate flexibility and a servant's attitude, which is one example I want my children to see modeled, because osmosis, I have come to realize, doesn't work precisely on kids.

As a husband and father, especially choosing to be a stay-at-home parent facing the responsibilities that go along with this choice, I hope its lasting effect on my children is to recognize the commitment and sacrifice it takes and learn by it.

Sports and the Boys

Doomed at a very young age to be a pretty slow runner, with asthma thwarting me even further, I knew becoming a world-class athlete would be a stretch. Still, the other kids played, and I wanted to play too. As a youth, I played Pee Wee and Little League Baseball playing for the Plaza Giants and later the Crabiel Angels, Crabiel being the local funeral home. I sucked at basketball, but I tried. A single was a home run to me. Scoring a basket was a thrill, scoring two an oddity, and scoring three, well, I don't think that ever happened in a game. I loved board games and tennis, chess, and swimming. I loved the challenge. Oh, I loved to win. And if I did not, that didn't matter, because we could always reset the board or start again. Believe me. I played to win every time, but did not get racked out about it if it did not turn in my direction. Ribbons were few and far between. I told you about my first trophy in acting.

I led my parents down roads they never imagined, and now my children are delivering doses of my own medicine. Permit me, if you will, to expound upon my children for a brief interlude. Frenetic as life can swell into, giving opportunities to my kids and being active with them provides the making of and, sometimes, the fulfillment of dreams. Here are a few stories and lessons from their lives.

Jamie played Little League Baseball. He tried hard and developed into a pretty good ballplayer. I would pitch to him in the backyard, and he hit everything I threw to him. I looked at it as him being a fine hitter rather than me being a lousy pitcher. When he did get a chance to play, he often had a good showing. He hustled, always giving it his all. He loved playing and hated losing. One baseball season, he played for the Bulldogs. You may remember the very popular song chant down in Georgia, "Who let the dogs out? Who? Who? Who?" One day, while watching the boys practice, I thought of a cute, silly, little ditty that spoofed that chant. Laughingly, I wrote a very nonintimidating tune that had the lyrics "There's a bulldog in the house. Hootie! Hootie!" So I would start singing this thing at the games whenever a kid would get a hit or we would score a run or something eventful happened in the game. The other parents would look at me as if I were nuts. My kids would not want to be anywhere around because it embarrassed them. One of the fathers asked me what I thought I was doing as we chatted behind the bleachers. I told him it's an experiment, telling him that by the end of the season, the folks in the stands would all be singing "There's a bulldog in the house. Hootie! Hootie!" with as much gusto as I had been doing (and telling my kids the same thing so they did not think I was completely nuts). I maintained a straight face while singing this (not easy) as if I were quite serious in this whole matter. Within a few games, some of the other parents started to join in with me, and by the end of the season I had everyone on our side doing their part. I still laugh at that one.

It might be worth repeating Jamie hated to lose. Whether it was bowling or learning to roller-skate, he could not understand how the pins didn't go down or how the floor kept coming up to meet him. But he worked and soon became pretty good at those too. He had his trials and triumphs. He played football and baseball and ran track in high school. If you saw the movie *Rudy*, about a kid with all heart and a work ethic that put the bigger, talented athletes to shame, that's Jamie. He came back from a concussion, maybe two, and a broken wrist to keep competing. The football team played in the state championship game one of his years losing by only two points with the winning catch only inches out of reach on the last play of the game.

Though the football team fell short in the championship game, his baseball team came through and won the state championship. As much as he loved playing baseball, he hung up his cleats to spend more time studying so he could earn a college scholarship. That was a difficult decision, but he made it. He won the scholarship, by the way, worth about $30,000. Beth and I think he made a wise choice.

Jeremy played baseball mostly because his older brother did. When he did get into a game, you could count on it to be in the outfield. The clouds in the sky seemed very interesting to him during these games, swatting at bugs too. He wasn't a bad player, just a bit distracted. Years later he played some soccer in high school and enjoyed that. Jeremy's talent is in the arts. Everything he did or does exudes creative energy. Sports may not have been his cup of tea, but he is an artist through and through. Acting, designing, and drawing sparked a lot of interest in him. We signed him up for lessons to develop them.

Joshua loves sports. He played Pop Warner football, organized basketball, and Pee Wee and Little League Baseball. As a youngster, basketball appeared too quick a game for him, struggling to keep up. Looking to me for help wouldn't get him too far anyway, so I didn't inspire him in any way here. Baseball proved much better to his liking, loving to play catcher and pretty darn good. In football, it helped to be a husky kid, unlike both Jamie and Jeremy, so he lined up on the offensive and defensive lines. He won a championship trophy one year playing for the 49ers. In high school, he concentrated his efforts on planting, establishing and building churches, playing drums in worship bands, doing mission work, and acting. His senior year football team had him again playing line on both sides of the ball. And playing the part of "Lurch" in the high school musical *The Addams Family: The Musical* would stand out as a highlight for a long time.

Because I took care of the kids and Hermie and Douglas, time didn't allow me to coach a team, except for one year, soon after my in-laws had passed away. The local roller rink had a roller hockey league, and they needed a coach. I volunteered. There are politics in all of these leagues, and this was no different. I did not really care. The other coaches took the experienced players and gave me every kid who had never played before because I was the new coach on the block. Any boy or girl who wanted to play, but never had, ended up on my team. Typically the teams were put in divisions according to experience with mine in the novice division. Kids up to fourteen years old who had never played before were going against seven-year-olds who had some experience already. In this way, I got to be the coach for Jamie, Jeremy, and Joshua on the same team.

It mattered little to me whether we won or lost, something the other coaches cared very highly about. Those days of suffering through my kids riding the bench only to sit and watch all the other kids throughout all those years get to play in the game, I now had the chance to do what I thought would be the best way to inspire these kids. I told my players that it did not matter if they won or lost, wanting them just to play and learn the game and, above all else, to have fun. Everyone would play in every game. It's not just for a few minutes but going in and out of the game constantly. I told them if they thought they were out of the game too long, they should come and tug on my shirt to substitute them back in. We did not have a goalie, so we had to borrow one from another team. It gave that kid a chance to get some extra game time. The team won one game that year, lost twelve, and tied one. Those other teams would skate circles around my team, even my older ones. All I asked was that they do their best and they would get better. My boys still tell me it's the greatest season they ever had (except Jeremy, who holds his bowling team above this). Had we not moved, I am sure we could have won at least one more game the next year. Then again, maybe not! The chance to play, the chance to get better, and finding joy in that, not on the outcome, far outweighed the win or loss record. There would always be time for that later.

My father came to see me play in one soccer game and one or two gymnastics meets. To be fair, I do not remember him missing any concerts, plays, or musicals whenever he could. Fortunately, Dad knew how much I appreciated his support.

We attend almost all of their games, concerts, plays, and programs. I ready the kids for the activities. Beth needs only to show up for the events on most occasions. Yet, of course, Beth takes her share of the many tasks as well. With the demands of the family not always lining up in perfect unison, we are drawn in different directions many times to accommodate the schedule. As I have said before, raising children is really a partnership of the first order, and coordination requires communication and cooperation. Seeing how responsibility is shared by members of a baseball team or any team, our children could see that the same is true for a family.

Little Miss Vidalia

The fabric of Jenna's first four years produced a tapestry woven by a chaotic mix of commotion. We had moved and were taking care of her grandparents. The boys were in full swing with their sports activities, sweeping Jenna up and loading her almost as part of the equipment. Enrolling her in preschool gave me a couple of hours to do necessary chores. Like her brothers, she had energy, a lot of it. Folks would ask where she got all of that energy.

To which I replied, "From me! She is taking mine!" She stood squarely in the center of the vortex, while the world revolved around her, the whirlwind a natural state of being, all normal in her eyes. It seemed the ions of a room changed when she entered it. Jenna commanded attention and not negatively so. There is a presence about her. From my years in the spotlight, I knew when someone had that presence about them. Maybe this is something that can be developed and that may occur. I am more of the mind that it is a gift that one is born with. Of course it can be squelched as any talent or gift can be. How many are never encouraged with theirs because conditions don't allow or have hindered that. Not every seedling grows just because it is planted. Not every plant will survive and flourish just because it is watered. Care must be administered to children with the same love that a magnificent garden is likewise nurtured.

Jenna displayed a high level of confidence from the very beginning. On her return from her first day of preschool, she recited her newly learned Bible verse, "In the beginning, God created the Heavens and the Earth" (Genesis 1:1). It came out as this: "In the beginning, God be crated the Heavens and the Earth. Jenna says 1:1." That pretty much said it all.

A few years later, when living in Vidalia, Georgia, Beth entered Jenna into the Little Miss Vidalia pageant. She had been taking dance lessons for a while. We learned about the contest from other parents.

Pageants, we discovered, were usually either a "natural" competition, meaning not made up to any great extent, or a "glitz" pageant with heavy makeup and wigs and lots and lots of sparkles on the extravagant dresses. Some went so far as to create a porcelain doll persona. Jenna always competed in the least makeup "natural" events. There were different age groups as well. While waiting for her first pageant to begin, Jenna befriended a fellow competitor. As the facilitators called Jenna's age category backstage to prepare for the competition, she sat with her new friend; took hold of both her hands; looked her in the eyes, knees to knees; and said with all sincerity and all encouragement possible, "I sure hope you come in second!" In Jenna's mind, Jenna owned first place, and second place would be the very best thing that she could wish for anybody else. Jenna did win her age group and became Little Miss Vidalia.

Jenna won her next pageant as well. After that she never took top prize but received numerous other honors, riding in parades and making the paper. Having had the early successes, we never felt it to be a driving force to have to win another pageant, but nice if she did. It bothers me that so many mothers take this so seriously and apparently to feed their own ego. I learned that as the girls get older, scholarship money goes along with each win, so I can see why some go this route. Criticism comes too with the pageant image that characterized JonBenet Ramsey.

Most of the fathers I met during these pageants would have rather been anywhere else than in a theater on a Saturday morning and afternoon. I could relate to that too, but I wanted to support Beth and Jenna. Actually, seeing the few men there made me wonder where the rest of the dads were. After the fourth one, I had had my fill, but still attended. There would be only a handful more to go to as it turned out. Promises that a pageant would be a "natural" event but turned out to be a "glitz" pageant happened too many times. Judging would bias in favor of the glitz, usually making it an uneven playing field. Without going to the "glitz" pageants, the "natural" ones were not as prevalent.

Our purpose in finding something more feminine and not sports related materialized here providing a totally different focus for our daughter. It did teach her poise on stage among other performance lessons. Our philosophy of trying new and different things has always been evident in giving the kids a chance to experience something and then allowing them to continue or not.

Oh, we all get run over once in our lives. But one must pick oneself up again. And behave as if it were nothing.

—Henrik Ibsen

CHAPTER
11

PRESSURE

Owning a Business, Losing a Business

Calculated risk is an interesting expression. We know risk is involved, and calculated is a word that sort of gives permission to take that risk, because it infers that there has been some process of evaluation in the decision. We weigh the facts of the matter, come to some kind of a conclusion, and act on it or let the situation proceed without us. Small circumstances are routine and usually carry no real danger of causing massive upheaval if they fall through. The big ones like buying a car and a house, a business, or investment can be a huge gamble. But if it is calculated, then odds of a bad outcome are lessened. Risk is still involved, but if all works favorably, the danger of loss is mollified by a potential gain.

From the time Beth and I had our children, we knew that when they were old enough, we would look for a business opportunity for me to work. It is why we worked at the Amway business for a while. We explored many different types of businesses over the years. We owned property thinking this would work to secure our future. The goal was to build a business so that Beth could reduce her schedule if she chose to down the road.

Along came an opportunity to get in on a franchise business with a great business model showing great success in a field that showed great potential. Everything about it looked positive. After careful thought and proper research, we bought into the business. I opened a clinic two hours away from our home and hired competent people to run the day-to-day operation. I monitored much of the activity by computer from home.

In the beginning, I dropped the kids off at school and had them in after-school activities, allowing me to travel up to the clinic and take care of setting things up. I put the advertising plan in place and worked on the radio advertising, the magazine ads, and other promotional plans. The drive through rural Georgia gave me time to make business calls that needed to be made.

Everything looked great guns but our sales. They just never seemed to match our projections with the age-old case of more money going out than coming in. I had a manager who did everything well except sell. Something had to be done. Too much time had gone by, and we could not tolerate the insipid growth. Other clinics produced, and ours should have had similar results. Finally, I needed to make a switch and hired a new manager. Within a month and a half, we exceeded projections and never looked back. Each month, our sales surpassed the target numbers. Our new manager knew how to close a sale, and the morale in the clinic responded positively. The only problem that now remained was to pay down the debt accumulated in carrying the clinic for those many months before the turnaround.

I set a payment plan up but made extra payments to lower my credit card debt. And as I paid down the cards, the credit card companies started lowering the credit limits. This was given only passing thought since I wanted to get out of debt completely.

The main corporation at this time offered to buy back some of their franchises in hopes of having a larger corporation buy them out. By having more clinics in the corporate fold, it presented a larger profit margin. Corporate came to us and offered to buy us out. The terms they offered were on the low side with payment to be in installments over three years, so we thought that after a few more months like we were having, an adjusted offer would be more to our liking. After all, we had weathered a rough beginning and were finally getting the ball rolling, going so well, in fact, that there were discussions of opening another clinic. So we turned down their offer.

The clinic continued breaking records, and I continued paying down loans and credit cards rapidly, not saving a lot of cash, just paying debt. And each time, the limits were reduced. I did wonder why this happened, but did not see the entire spectrum of finance shrinking. I did not read the signs. The banks knew a financial crunch was looming, so in 2008, banks pulled back and shrunk available credit, and this included me. The bubble had popped with the multitude scrambling to keep things going. Our sales became inconsistent suddenly. I had just made large debt payments with no worries, based on recent sales trends. Sales fell off dramatically, putting me in a cash crunch. A couple of other unforeseen wrinkles came up, but the timing could not have been worse. Besides sales being off, a reversal of a large contract resulting in a credit card company dispute saw money removed from my account without notice, causing a few checks to bounce. The amount of money I am talking about, to put this in perspective, equaled about three to four days of sales, but enough to throw things into a complete kerfuffle.

I requested from corporate the grace of a few days to make payment on a royalty check I owed them. They refused and told me if I did not have the money to them by Thursday at 5:00 p.m., they would close me down and take over the business. Those few wrinkles were now a tsunami. They locked me out and took over my accounts. I could go more into detail here, but the gist of the matter is this: Because we turned down their offer to buy us out six months prior, they looked for and found any reason they could to take us over. Our refusal to sell put a target on our heads. My clinic now reached number ten in the nation out of seventy clinics. It stood as number two in the stand-alone single clinic market locations by only a few thousand dollars.

The next day, I phoned my lawyers and spoke to them from the State Capital Building in Atlanta, Georgia, where my daughter's artwork, chosen from across Georgia, was displayed in a main gallery of the building, with the parents, teachers, and children attending the ceremonies. Between my calls, we met the state senators and congressmen from our district. What an honor for Jenna. I smiled graciously on the outside, but inside I felt like a horse kicked me in the stomach. Disbelief covered the feeling pretty well.

What they had done was illegal. They did not have the right to take me without allowing me to cure the problem. We had thirty days to do so, and I had a case against them, but no money to fight them. We tried to get them to the arbitration process, but the offers were practically worthless as they employed delay tactics. They could afford to. We could not. Even if we did get to arbitration and won, any money attained would be eaten up by lawyer fees and new debt. So we just walked away sustaining losses in the two million-dollar category.

Fighting guaranteed no positive outcome except perpetuating a constant state of distress. It had to be evaluated. What would be lost and what would be gained? We felt that our health to be more important. I would rather work on building a future than to try and fix an unfixable past. We had to move forward. The anger and frustration had to be put aside. The tsunami hits, the hurricane slams, and the tornado destroys. Lives are shattered, and the aftermath needs to be cleaned up. Business is a treacherous world affording great possibilities yet with a downside equally as destructive a force as nature can produce.

Corporations don't really care to take over a struggling franchise I discovered. They will if it means saving their reputation. I learned the hard way that they would much prefer to pick the plum.

The signs of a depression crept up with only the astute noticing. Although I did notice the banks changing my credit agreements, I didn't understand the ramifications and what it all heralded. Subsequently, and too late I might add, I read that in the 1920s the banks did not want to take over the houses with large mortgages or the businesses that were failing. No, they were much more interested in the homes that were almost completely paid off or businesses for the most part solvent but had run up against the same thing I had just run into, poor cash flow that led to acute distress and not able to meet a short-term crunch. It made more sense for lending institutions and banks to repossess the properties with a higher level of equity than the ones that only produced more debt, something that could be saved not the ones deeply in a hole.

Within a few months we lost all of our property, two homes and some land. I sold our silver and gold to jump-start a new beginning in a new town, while my wife took a new position. Bankers, lawyers, building contractors, friends, and relatives were not immune to this crash. It knocked out billions with one big sucker punch.

Second-guessing in a situation like this only prolongs the anguish. You know the "what ifs" drive you crazy. My son Jamie said something to me that stopped the self-flogging for being a poor businessman.

"Any man who can build a business to a million-and-a-half dollars a year in a three-year span is a success. You are a success, Dad. A banker isn't a failure because his bank gets robbed, and neither are you," Jamie said encouragingly.

Jamie, while being completely correct, took the negative situation and refocused me to the positive accomplishments I did attain. Those words from my son, at that time, felt like he lifted me up from the canvas, dusted me off, wiped my gloves, and sent me back into the world, to fight another day.

What had happened to us? It's nothing that hadn't happened to thousands and thousands across the country at that time! We were not alone in losing just about everything. That knowledge only gave us perspective of the situation and no real relief. We knew others were going through hell as well, and that could not provide any sense of comfort. "Misery loves company" is the saying. To me, this only means that empathy among the aggrieved can see that the blame of their situation is not entirely their own fault. Sure, there will always be a portion of culpability applied. Life is a risk, and sometimes we are surprised that we are exposed in that risk. And sometimes we are devastated by the results of a risk, no matter how many contingencies are covered. If there is no risk in something, everyone would have a stake.

Win or lose, nothing stays the same. The flow of a river does not stop because a rock gets in the way. Flowing with it is easier than trying to swim back upstream. The energy used to regain lost positions is pretty much futile. Even if you got back to the place you once were, the river has moved on, and you will have to face a new set of conditions and possibly a new flux.

Some careers end in a mere few years. Depending on which disciplines you look at, some are over by early to mid-twenties. Dancers, gymnasts, skaters, swimmers, and athletes, for example, have to move on sooner than they may wish to. Of course, injury causes an abrupt reevaluation and can end a career instantly.

Trauma in life comes in many packages and can't always be identified by its wrapper or when you must take delivery. Aside from the careers that carry the kinds of risks I just mentioned, there are other life-altering traumas that come into play from time to time. Studies show that moving, divorce, loss of a child, loss of a parent, loss of a job, a job change, bankruptcy, and illness are the greatest causes of stress in a person's life. If this is so, I am in big trouble. If you look at the list, most of those things are not totally in your control. With most of life's challenges, going around, over, or under them is rarely the option. They have to be dealt with by going head on, directly through them. Avoidance gives a problem the chance to fester into a more painful obstacle. This leads to more work to rectify what might have been at one time manageable to something akin to a ten-headed monster if you are not careful.

Breathing

The first thing that needs to be done when any on this list rears its ugly head is to breathe. And breathe deep. Breathing calms you down and allows you to think. The brain needs oxygen, and when under pressure there is a need to not panic.

Think back to the tough times in your life, and you may agree with me that trying to keep your breath proved a difficult task, almost like a forgotten art form. Even in relatively sanguine times, breathing is not done to its utmost benefit.

If you pay attention to your breathing patterns right now, you are most likely taking short shallow breaths. Try taking a deep breath right now and see how that makes you feel.

Breathe in deeply through your nose to the count of four filling your stomach like a balloon and breathe out through your mouth to the count of eight depleting the balloon. Repeat that a few times. Let your shoulders drop. This will help you relax your body. I hope that helps!

This is good when you are feeling tense. Try it when stopped at a red light or sitting home to clear your head. Try this before you start your day. Try this before you go to sleep. There is no bad time to breathe. Enjoying it once in a while is a pleasure.

We take breathing for granted because it is automatic. If you have ever had a good shot to the solar plexus that causes an interruption to this automatic process, everything else you were thinking about has taken a back seat in priorities for the time being. Breath is the most immediate need we have. You can live forty days without food and four days without water, but a mere four minutes without air on this Earth will answer any questions you had about an afterlife or any mystery about what comes next.

Why do I talk to you about breathing? Other than the obvious need for sustaining consciousness, the benefits to taking time to monitor your breathing patterns will give you a renewed sense of equilibrium. It may not solve the problem at hand but will give you a better starting point to approach the issue. Problems do not automatically go away. But giving attention to relaxing the tension, even for a few moments, will better equip you to plan your next choice.

The Internal Revenue Service (IRS) and the B Word

When the dominoes began to topple, we did what we could to try to regain our footing. Quicksand is not a very stable foundation. Trying to save ourselves from declaring bankruptcy by short selling our home acted in the same way quicksand does. The more one tries to do, the more futile it seems. Compounding our dilemma was an equity line of credit attached to the house. Payments reduced the obligation down, but still we owed a substantial amount. One offer to buy the discounted house came in, but the bank holding the equity loan that sat in second position would receive only $5000.00 of the short sale, a small fraction of the actual loan amount. The sale required their approval. This did not happen, and instead the house went to auction on the courthouse steps. Now that bank received nothing. Laws in cases similar to this transaction put us in the obligation to report the difference of the sale price from the total amount of the mortgage and equity line amounts to be reported as taxable income. After much heartache, we had no alternative anymore and declared bankruptcy.

The process that this entails is humbling to say the least. We delayed going to this solution by trying to dig out from under and just could not. In a "Hail Mary" attempt and with connections in Los Angeles, I even took the kids there to audition for television shows in hopes of landing commercial jobs or television work. Just when things were starting to look a bit promising, Beth's position with the hospital was eliminated with one week's notice. I now homeschooled three of the kids because of the audition process in Los Angeles. That lasted about a semester, and I reenrolled them back into the school system once we knew for sure we were going to be staying. Jeremy did not want to go back for a half of a year and decided to just get his GED, which he did. Weeks of time were spent gathering documents to accommodate the requirements for the bankruptcy over the next many months.

Simultaneously, we were locked in a battle with the Internal Revenue Service over disputed taxes and filings. It turned out for a period of two years in the early 2000s, our CPA had failed to send in our returns, and that had to be straightened out as well. We could not understand why we were getting notices and had asked about them, but nothing seemed to be resolving the issues. It's not until we were gathering the information for the bankruptcy did we discover the error. When the IRS does not receive a filing, they use the documents that they do get (W-2s and others) and use that information as the basis of the filing. So there were no deductions or anything like that, just the amount reported to them as earned income according to their paperwork with that amount used to establish the tax liability.

Why do I reveal such personal interludes of our lives? It is because this is part of the whole picture. My experiences make me who I am today. Going through trials and tribulations is rarely welcome. More lessons are learned through adversity than times of comfort. That is the nature of it all. Contrast makes for richer experiences. Ease alone gets wearisome as do pain and suffering. So by telling you about some of my tougher times, maybe it will help you in some form or another.

While going through all of these things, life did not just stop and allow for the buttoning up of pressing issues. I still had to do the daily things a stay-at-home parent must do. Anyone who is still of the opinion that a stay-at-home parent sits idly by while the rest of the world works is, at this point, wholly delusional. Problems usually do not just disappear. They typically fester if not rectified. Laundry does not just automatically get clean. Dishes do not wash themselves. And the walls and doors of a house do not prevent aggravations, situations, complications, snags, and hitches from entering this life.

"When sorrows come, they come not
single spies, but in battalions!"

—William Shakespeare, *Hamlet*

CHAPTER
12

TURBULENCE

The Phone Call

When deciding to write this book, the initial thought for its subject revolved around my son. While gathering ideas and facts on paper and speaking to a friend, an author, about my intentions, she encouraged me to write, without hesitation, though she thought it would be wiser to expand the scope of it to telling my own story. It initially felt important to expound the story I am about to share with more detail and more of the characters, including interviews and perspectives of those I intended to include. Yet, she maintained that my son's story needed to be told but as a segment and not the dominating theme of the book. In heeding her advice, but wanting to touch on something that so many families have a direct or indirect connection to, I will describe a bit of this very bumpy road. Some parts of the parenting voyage carry with it unexpected detours. This is one such wind shift.

All slept peacefully in the still and quiet house on this cool still dark early Thursday morning, late November 2011. And it's not just any Thursday; it's Thanksgiving Thursday. At least, I thought all were sleeping. In the stillness of sleep, the phone rang. Now, if the phone rang in our house at odd times, it could not be construed as unusual because my wife is a doctor and calls come in at any time of the day or night. The phone sat in its holder near me, so I answered it fully expecting to hear the request to speak with Beth, then pass the phone over to Beth, and return to a semi-sleep while I listened to see if she needed to fly off to the emergency room. Grogginess is a pretty typical response of mine to a call at around 5:00 a.m.

Normally it is not a good thing for Beth to have to go in on an emergency, but usually the problem is handled with the patient being seen and treated or on occasion taken to the operating room. In any case, the problem is handled with a course of action for the patient by the doctor. Most times this would be a simple, short-term event. Other times required more care and commitment toward recovery.

None of those things manifested in such a way on this Thanksgiving morning. As I answered the phone, the voice on the other end did not ask for the doctor, but asked for me. He identified himself as a deputy in the sheriff's department in our local county and informed me that they arrested our son. He said the charges were numerous but included unlawful entry of vehicles, theft from the vehicles, drug possession, and gun possession. I bolted upright, stunned and now wide awake.

After being picked up by the police, Jeremy was now in their custody and not in any danger. The officer told me reassuringly he did not put anyone in danger and that he gave no resistance in the arrest, complying with the arresting officers. So our concern and fear of the worst news felt only slightly mitigated by not having to respond to a tragedy. We did not have the need to go to an accident scene, a hospital, or a morgue. That seemed the only blessing that morning. I know the things I just mentioned do occur, and all of those thoughts crossed my mind in the mere seconds that the officer took to lay out the situation. While thankful to not having heard the worst of news possible, we were no less shaken and concerned.

What had followed since that morning call had taken my family down roads and to places that I never could have imagined.

We received a call from our boy from jail, extremely apologetic and quite upset. Well, really, who wouldn't be? Our first questions to him were to ascertain the reasons he did these stupid things.

Jeremy had been accepted into a professional makeup school in Los Angeles, California. It would be expensive to attend, and because of our financial situation, he could not count on our immediate support to attend. We had not explored all options either for that to this point, planning to look at those options after Thanksgiving. He thought he could raise money instead by stealing and selling. I still don't know how he got to the point in his thinking that this offered him a viable and practical method. He didn't get this by our example. Short-term and immature thinking, drugs, impatience, and maybe outside influences led to his predicament. Unfortunately, he now found himself in a pickle.

I told him we would do what we could to find out all the information available and how we might help in the process.

There are parts of our society, sadly, that having a loved one incarcerated is not an uncommon event. In our case, his arrest dropped us squarely in the middle of an unknown culture and a surprisingly unexpected uncommon event.

The last few years had battered us. Hope had just begun to rise again after finishing the patchwork trying to repair the ripped fabric those past few years took us through. We barely had a chance to catch our breath when this came along and slammed us into what felt like a brick wall.

So, on this day where we all would wake up and enjoy the Thanksgiving Day Parade on television, while we all did something to prepare for our big meal, life altered the course of that day and many, many days to follow.

Beth and I went to the jail to see if we could visit with the new inmate and were told we needed to come back later, to provide him with white underwear, white tee shirts, and white socks, his "whites," no printing or color on any of them. We purchased the items at Walmart and then headed back home and opened up all of the "whites" and then labeled them with his initials using a permanent marker to mark them. Once Jeremy's predicament was explained to his siblings, the mood turned extremely somber, and whatever the plans to have a lovely day had been quickly and completely wiped away.

Returning to the jail, we went through a process that became routine in the following years presenting identification and being checked in for visitation. The sergeant on duty during that morning, by chance, happened to be the mother of two of Jeremy's friends from high school. Possibly without realizing it, she proved to be such a blessing in our lives. I suspect that because of her position in the system, Jeremy had extra eyes on him. I do not mean to infer that he got special treatment because I do not think that's the case, only that if any issue came up, we knew about it a little quicker.

In delivering the newly purchased, freshly marked shirts, socks, and underwear, the sergeant informed us that they would not be allowed because they were not in the original packaging. This would mean another trip to the store, more expense, and still more disruption. But since we were ignorant of the procedure, the requirement of new packaging was waived this once. It being Thanksgiving might have played into it too. It's a small thing, to be sure, but we certainly appreciated it just the same. And we would comply with this stipulation from that point on, although we did not know that there would be a next time at that point. In some ways this rule seemed ridiculous. As I would later find out, many rules seemed ridiculous. But they were in place not for the rational-thinking person. They were there to protect the ones running the correction center, the ones in the correction center, and the ones visiting the correction center. This was merely the beginning of our education into a world that we had never been part of and did not want to be a part of. For example, protocol for letters to inmates appeared a little far-reaching. Guards read incoming mail and removed the stamp from the envelope before passing it on the intended recipient. I found out the guards removed the stamp as a precaution because LSD had been found to be passed into the jail this way. One small illustration of things of this nature never crossed my mind before.

As the days unfolded, we saw that many who ended up behind bars rotated in and out of jail. This happened with a percentage of inmates who could not seem to get out of the system, for a host of reasons. Some of them returned because they had no support from friends or family. Some cycled in for probation or parole violations, and some did not learn from past experiences and recommitted crimes or committed new ones. Then some intentionally did things to be sent back because they had learned this culture and it made no difference to them where they spent their time, knowing what to expect and consequently giving them a break from the outside world. To many who have not lived their lives intersecting with this mentality, this seems a completely foreign concept. Why would anyone choose to give up their freedom? But that is how many have come to live. Through ignorance or stupidity or a bit of bad luck, many have found themselves cycling through the system. It certainly is a mind-set that perpetuates itself into a downward spiral if there is not a conscious decision to rectify this pattern. And even that is only the beginning of extraction from the grip that the law can and will impose. Wanting to change is always the start, but it will certainly not be enough to reroute the path that people will find themselves on.

We did not know these things yet, all this being new to us. We struggled to navigate the swirling emotions we faced and learned what we needed to do to handle this crisis. We kept saying that no one ended up dead and no one physically harmed and thus were relieved in that aspect. Our boy landed in trouble with the law. That thought alone upset us, but his treatment now became a real concern, as it would be from this time on.

At this time, because he was still in booking, they allowed a visit to see him live with only thick glass separating us, not the typical visitation procedure in the county correction center. Other facilities had different setups, but here the usual visit provided a booth with a phone looking at a monitor. Here there were eight booths hooked up to the different jail sections called pods, by camera, where the jailed were brought to their side of the monitor with the visitor in the main reception area of the jail. After checking in with a photo ID, one was then directed to one of the booths, waiting for the monitor connection and the visit to start. It was twice a week for a half hour at appointed times. We were quite fortunate to have visits with him through the glass over the following six weeks when we did get to visit. I found out these were the attorney visit booths, different because it allowed access, by a small access drawer, for important documents that needed to be signed.

Because Jeremy had not been let out of booking for the first three days, we had these visits in such a manner, probably because of the holiday weekend. They kept Jeremy in the medical unit, a separate area of the jail, after displaying actions that caused the guards to think he might be at risk for personal harm to himself. Scratching his wrist with his fingernails enough to cause it to bleed slightly and punching himself in the nose to cause it to bleed, Jeremy then smeared the blood on his wrist and let droplets fall to the floor to create the effect of a suicide threat. Later, Jeremy said this was a ploy to get him out of being placed in the general population of the jail, which he had great angst about, hoping this would lead to his being kept in the medical unit. And so he was, for his protection as well as theirs. He spent the next six weeks, until the beginning of January, in the med unit causing a whole new level of concern, as you might imagine.

His arrest came when we were in no financial position to do much of anything concerning the hiring of a lawyer, after going through a total reorganization that strapped us at that time. Hiring a lawyer would have been a great idea, but finances did not allow us to, leaving us little choice having to proceed with a public defender. With the bail set at $45,000 and bond nearly $6000, Jeremy would sit in jail for a while. And, of course, because of the holiday weekend, nothing would be done for days at that stage.

In reality, even without making the bond, we only had about two weeks to try to negotiate his release; but because his actions aggravated his plight, Jeremy ran into the system full force.

During the night of his spree, Jeremy entered unlocked cars and rummaged through them looking for things to sell or pawn. He found a loaded gun under the seat of one of the cars. Removing the bullets he slipped them into his pocket and stashed the pistol in his bag. The sheriff's deputies confronted Jeremy and found the weapon in his possession. For their own protection, they treated this as a serious possible threat to their own safety, although Jeremy never brandished the gun in any way. How he came to acquire it did not matter to them at that moment.

The mere fact that he possessed the pistol upon arrest gave law enforcement enough to charge him with that crime. We would later, after a few lengthy discussions with the prosecutor, resolve that issue once it was established that he had it as a result of the spree and not part of the commission of his escapade.

Ultimately, that charge got dropped. If it were not, a more severe punishment could be pronounced because it carried a higher level of felony weight.

So for Thanksgiving weekend, Jeremy spent his time waiting for something to happen. Nothing would happen. He would sit. Offices were closed for the holiday weekend.

We taught him better. He knew better. Letting him sit and stew for the weekend to consider his actions until we could work to straighten things out and face the situation on the following Monday might be a good idea.

Parenting in these conditions takes on a whole new realm of choices. And some of those choices are now taken away from the parents when put into the hands of the legal system, almost as if to say, "Parents, you screwed up. Now it's our turn. We know better than you do."

Certainly, anger bubbled over about his stupid choices. Any underlying emotions were needed to be quelled for the time being. Navigating through this quagmire of a system became our front-burner priority.

What promised to be a fun and enjoyable weekend deflated into a dark and uncomfortable pall. Thoughts could not be diverted away from the jail. The only real relief from this upset came saying it could have been worse, not to minimize the arrest, but to merely try to keep things in a certain perspective. Our kid screwed up, and life would move forward with an altered course. Lives do that. They change course by choices. If only this were a story of an immature eighteen-year-old jumping head first into a nasty, tangled briar patch. No, his problems were more hampering.

I discovered how far-reaching and how many lives would be touched by Jeremy's actions because of that one night. How many hours, days, weeks, months, and now years had been altered because of this simple crime. And this is just one little episode with one young man doing something he should not have been doing, in places he should not have been. When I think of the world in general and how many of these types of occurrences set off chains of events that drive so many people off their own course every moment of every day, it astounds my senses.

How many people now have to respond to a new condition set in place by a negative act, in this instance, and how does it affect people? The victims now have their world affected. They have to deal with loss of property. The law officers have new work in front of them, from the patrolman to the many officers in the jail and later the court system with the attorneys and the court personnel and all the unexpected things that occur in response from that day forward. It alters choices and conditions that cannot be measured. It's their job. And it is an extensive job force working in this system: from the police at the front of this picture to the correction facility guards, clerks, nurses, and kitchen workers; then to the public defenders, lawyers, prosecutors, and all the secretaries; and then onto the court with all the personnel running that organization. This is only on the local level. It moves on to the regional and the state levels and then to the federal levels. It is our legal system, a confoundedly great morass to the uninitiated. From its lower levels to the higher ones, chaos prevails even with the best attempts to sort out the frivolous from the severe. My point here is that the path that our son had swerved upon would take much time on many people's schedules finding a way to either keep him stuck in the quagmire or too busy in the labyrinth, all this so that the energy expended would give enough of a deterrent from crime as possible and therefore the punishment would have its desired effect. The process itself is a part of that punishment.

In thinking about Jeremy's foolish night and its ramifications, it becomes crystal clear that his actions did affect others. The ripple effect was abundantly evident.

We want everything in its place for greater ease. At least, most of us want a calm serenity. It is our basic instinct to smooth the wrinkled, soothe the sore, and fix the broken. Yet there are those who will go against this causing discord.

Society has put in place these checks and balances. Many, many people who are charged with the righting of wrongs have found their places in a system that is designed to remove the wrinkles.

The Public Defender

Jeremy sat behind bars in the medical unit of the correction center, with the jail on alert to his potential to do harm to himself. The ripples he created filtered into the decision making of the court. Since drugs were found at the time of arrest, it qualified him for a program called drug court. The two-year rehabilitation was needed to be successfully completed to have all charges expunged to reflect no lingering record to deal with.

After talking with the public defender, first offender status, which would be less forgiving if the conditions of probation were violated which meant that conviction would proceed with a harsher outcome, could also be considered.

Jeremy exacerbated his situation by the wrist incident. But it opened the door to a program called help court, which added a psychological need component to the drug court program. Both were virtually the same in all aspects with an added layer of lee-way for the court to use. If not completed satisfactorily, sentencing from the original charges would occur and would have to be served out.

Unfortunately, help court, offered in the county next to us, not ours, had to be coordinated between the two counties. The fast-approaching holidays compounded the problem with most of the legal system coming to a halt during that time.

After all of the wrangling and evaluations, help court would be a viable option, but required that Jeremy would remain jailed until the next court date of January 6.

Not at all familiar with the process, having a child in jail caused us to ache from the anguish and uncertainty throughout this period of time.

The Court

Jeremy had to be transferred with sentencing taking place in the neighboring county.

Jeremy entered the courtroom in his orange jumpsuit with arm and leg cuffs on, along with others who were there for similar reasons, all seating in the jury box and creating an orange tableau. He looked our way. With a little nod of his head, half smile, and sad forlorn eyes that expressed both relief in seeing us and regret for landing in this position, he sat waiting for the judge to appear.

The current participants sat intermingled in the general court area over the next two hours as the judge went through each one's weekly progress. Some were praised, and some were reprimanded. Good behavior sometimes was rewarded by a candy bar or gift certificate of five to ten dollars for a local restaurant. A poor week could elicit added community service or even a return to jail for a varied length of time depending on the frequency and severity of the infractions. The judge listened and, although seemingly understanding, did not give in to the remorse of the participants.

In order to be admitted to the program, the charged individual must agree to the terms of the release and plead guilty to the charges they were arrested for, which were then sealed and put aside until completing the program. Once satisfying the conditions and requirements fully, the charges would be forever expunged.

The idea of the program, from my perspective, seemed to be a viable option. It offered a way for Jeremy to stay out of jail while getting back on track.

The Letters

Communication during this time allowed only letters, a few phone calls, and twice-a-week half-hour visitations. Because they kept him in the medical unit, they allowed him to call more often.

Phone calls were made by purchasing prepaid phone cards or signing up for a less expensive but still costly phone service that was approved by the folks in the legal system. One phone call would usually be limited to ten to twenty minutes. Calls made by reversing the charges cost even higher still.

Money deposited into the inmates' account by money orders or other guaranteed monies for their use in the commissary allowed them to purchase shampoo, candy, snacks, instant coffee, pencils, paper, stamps, envelopes, and even a tiny transistor radio—all at inflated prices! The costs were borne by the families and friends of the inmate. Very few had money of their own. So just for some basic things, the costs could add up over a period of time.

This is maybe just another set of reasons to keep out of jail.

Hearing a voice can be assuring in circumstances like these. Expensive or not, it can calm the anxiety. As with everything concerning the jail and its system of procedures, life is disrupted. Schedules now are adjusted to be available at certain times of certain days to receive a call or for visitation. Getting the calls or going to visitation offers some type of reassurance but seems to always be too short or insufficient. To those unfamiliar with this, and we certainly were not familiar, I tell you that each occurrence carried with it an unpleasant emptiness. In writing this, the underlying sadness that circled then still remains. With us, hopes were that this would not be a long endurance on ours or Jeremy's part. But for many, this drags on for many years.

By writing letters, I expected to say things more succinctly. Thoughts rolled through my head at a rapid pace, and sometimes, by the time the discussion subject had passed, I'd have new thoughts on the current flow of the conversation. Letters allowed me to write down, without interruption, my thoughts in a methodical way. And as Jeremy sat in jail, my letters were written rather frequently, expressing to him my love and concern for him. I wrote to guide, teach, encourage, and warn him. Writing afforded that my thoughts could be put down in some cohesive manner.

The wise man in the storm prays to God, not for safety from danger, but deliverance from fear. (Ralph Waldo Emerson)

The Unpredictable Routine

In order to be admitted into the drug court program, papers have to be signed giving up certain rights. These are under the fourth amendment rights in the Constitution regarding search and seizure, privacy laws, and things of that nature. As I mentioned earlier, the admission of guilt is signed and sealed only to be unsealed if the participant fails to complete the program, in which case the judge will have the authority to pass sentence on the offenses. Giving up the right to a trial by jury is one of the conditions that were agreed to in the initial paperwork.

The legal and judicial systems are a maze of intricacies to someone not familiar with the layered processes that are in place. The elements of this particular drug court program are designed to keep the participants from "playing" the system. Random drug testing, job search requirements, community service, AA meeting, Narcotics Anonymous meetings, counseling meetings and sessions, weekly court appearances, curfews and visits from the sheriff's office to the home with the option of a search without a warrant (remember the fourth amendment waiver) to verify compliance to the curfew, and other breaches of the agreement are all utilized to refocus the participants, keeping them from falling back into old patterns that got them into the mess they are in to begin with.

Complying with these stipulations and satisfying the conditions would, after the two-year program, allow each to walk away without a conviction on their record, many of them felonies, carrying a much more serious status with many more long-term ramifications than the lesser offenses.

I wish I could tell you here that Jeremy made it through and life went on a rosy path for him and for us. It did not. The random drug testing he had to comply with started every day with a phone call at 5:30 a.m. to see if he was to report to the testing center (a half-hour away). If he had to report for the urine test, he had to be there between 7:00 a.m. and 7:50 a.m. If he did not report, the court allowed one opportunity to report later that day at 5:00 p.m. If he missed, he would go back to jail for a day. Each subsequent miss would be a longer jail penalty. If the participant could not produce the urine for the test, that would be considered a missed test and would then mean a need to go to jail for the penalty. The penalty would be meted out during the Friday drug court session by the judge.

In the beginning of the program, the randomness would occur more often, from three to four times a week and designed to curtail defiance of the rules.

Jeremy could not pee in the cup one time as the officer watched and subsequently returned to jail for the one night. On the second occasion, he would be sent for two nights. Pressure of having to pee on command with a hulking officer eyeing the entire process can cause most anyone to have trouble producing the specimen. This happened to Jeremy on one particular occasion. As time ran out, he had only filled the cup half way, and in the midst of finishing, the officer denied him the decency to conclude the required amount. Now considered a breach, Jeremy would have to pay the penalty being sent back to jail for a two-night stay. Jeremy tried to comply but was denied a level of sensibleness for whatever power play the officer decided to wield in this situation. That same day a friend of Jeremy's had committed suicide adding to his own upset.

On the Thursday night before the Friday drug court session, Jeremy swallowed four bottles of cough medicine capsules containing dextromethorphan, a sedative. In trying to rouse him from bed for the 5:30 a.m. drug screen call, I found him nearly unresponsive and utterly incoherent. I looked in the bathroom trashcan and saw the empty bottles. Beth and I took him immediately to the emergency room. Having vomited most of the capsules up during the night, we later found out, resulted from a chemical in the plastic capsule itself that induces the body to reject large quantities. Nonetheless, he had his stomach pumped for anything still in his system. Once out of danger, the admitting doctor transferred him to the psychiatric unit of the hospital. We requested that his condition and hospitalization be told to the drug court and judge, and they reassured that this would be done. It was not done, and the judge issued a bench warrant ordering for Jeremy's arrest designating immediate jail time to last until the next drug court session. Once the court found out Jeremy had gone to the hospital, they decided that he would be taken from there straight to jail. The doctor assured us he would not be released from the hospital until at least Tuesday. But for some reason, they released him to the police on Monday, before I could talk with anyone in drug court regarding his condition. Jeremy was ripped from the care of a hospital and thrown into a high-security, stripped-down cell and given only a paper gown to wear, with no blanket or sheets. Already in a fragile state of mind, he was now being treated like a dog and under a suicide watch. I did get to talk with him over the phone. He sounded quite distraught and emotional. Is this the help court acting in full compassion? Here is a young man taken from hospital care for attempting to take his own life, and the court could not delay its power until finding out all of the facts of the matter. After many phone calls to the staff of drug court, that Wednesday the judge held a closed-circuit monitor meeting with Jeremy. Determining Jeremy had understood his reprimands, the judge allowed me to take him home with me on the condition of being in drug court on Friday.

Between my picking Jeremy up and Friday's court session, conversations with the drug court prosecutor produced a court-approved sanction for Jeremy to go to a rehab facility to get treatment and that his participation in drug court would be temporarily suspended until he got out of rehab.

This saga continued. Jeremy completed the rehab, rejoined drug court, broke some rules, and spent a couple of weeks in jail that summer. After being out he rebelled against us as well, ran away and found himself arrested in Atlanta, transferred back, and subsequently terminated from drug court. He failed the drug court process and was sentenced to a year in jail with four years of probation for the conviction of his original charges. Probation also came with drug testing and periodic visits to a probation officer.

We had him apply to a technical school, and Jeremy was granted permission to attend while serving a month and a half on house arrest with an ankle monitor keeping track of his whereabouts instead of in jail. If he deviated from the scheduled locations and times, there would be calls made and reports to file.

The jail added a home charge, and the ankle monitor, provided for by an outside company, came with a daily charge as well. Both were needed to be paid in advance, or re-incarceration was imminent. Again, it was another chance to inflict a financial burden. And, if possible, many will try to bear it for their unfortunate loved one.

With a felony record now, having him learn a skill would be useful to him and was the reason we got him into a tech school, because finding a job would be difficult with a record. Many things are affected with a felony record to contend with. Renting an apartment of any quality or getting a loan becomes a major problem as a convicted felon.

Why do I include this unflattering portrait of a family heartbreak?

I assume most parents are taken by surprise when something like this occurs. We do not plan for such troubles. Situations involving the law, accidents, injuries, divorce, death, and all the other unpleasant conditions disrupt our families. This is when parenting takes on so much more than ever anticipated, regardless of our preconceived perceptions. In our case we now wrestled with Jeremy's legal entanglements.

Temptations to find a shortcut cross all walks of society. The lure of something for nothing or for little effort is appealing to those who do not have and want or have and want more. Blame can be speculated about, but I think there are so many influences contributing to the makeup of this attraction. It might be fruitless to find only one cause. What led to my son's choices through this period I am not sure. His mother and I have displayed and taught the value of hard work. We taught him the same principles as we had to our other children, yet he chose to rebel against what he knew to be right leading him into situations that could only be described as a quagmire, the ramifications of which would influence, if not his entire life, most definitely many years into his future.

Jesus said in a parable that if one of the shepherd's sheep was lost, the shepherd would leave the ninety-nine to go find the lost sheep. In my case, I never left my three to find my one. I did not need to do so in the same way. I did have to divert my time and energy away from my other children. My son hit a very rough patch. What message would that send to my other children if Beth and I left Jeremy to go it alone when he needed help? To me, the value of my child would be worth whatever work it took to get him onto a productive path. By this example, Jamie, Joshua, and Jenna know what it means to go beyond what seems fair. Hopefully, unconditional love has been displayed. And if it isn't unconditional, maybe just love would suffice. This does not mean I gave up my right to chastise and disapprove. Jeremy did wrong. He took things that he should not have, got caught, and had paid a steep price.

His story is not far from the story of Jean Valjean in Victor Hugo's *Les Miserables*. Jean Valjean stole a loaf of bread to feed his sister and children and was arrested, convicted, and sentenced to five years in prison. A sentence extended to almost twenty years because of his attempted escapes. Even after released from prison, he would be dogged by an unforgiving prefect bent on bringing him back to prison for breaking the rules of parole. Because a priest showed kindness and understanding, Valjean transformed his life and dedicated it to living righteously, his past always on the cusp of being uncovered.

No matter what we do for Jeremy, it will always be his decision to flow with the current or swim against it. And so it is with all of us, really. We pray for his wisdom in confronting and overcoming any and all of his challenges.

Wisdom is the principal thing; therefore get wisdom:
and with all thy getting get understanding.

—Proverbs 4:7

CHAPTER
13

SEEKING WISDOM

The Prodigal Son

Similar to the forgiveness of the priest in Hugo's tome, I have chosen to forgive my son. This does not mean that I condoned his actions or that continued disregard to the law would be acceptable. Perpetual punishment for past transgressions does no one any good. Forgiveness is a very difficult posture to assume and remember. The disputes that manifest in my own mind had me at odds with myself in trying to figure out how to best handle subsequent situations with Jeremy. Do I say something here? Do I chastise? Do I rebuke? Do I console and guide? How much tough love is enough? How do I keep from harping and lecturing? Only because my boy had gotten into trouble to this extent was this internal wrangling so pervasive. Balance and fairness are always grappled with. Of course, the other children had me twisting over what to allow or deny as well. Boundaries are always pushed.

Parenting as the children grow older demands less physical energy and more mental energy. The early days of child-rearing were filled with carrying, loading, lifting, and hauling. Generally, the kids would listen because we were bigger than them.

"Because I said so!" doesn't carry the weight it did when the children were younger. Every reason needs to be justified, or so it seems. Like equalizing the gifts at Christmas, rules among the kids have to have some semblance of equality.

"Why can't I go? You let him go?" Questions such as these dance in my head but step on my toes. Are my denials more to control than to protect?

The Parable of the Lost Son

Jesus continued: "There was a man who had two sons. The younger one said to his father, 'Father, give me my share of the estate.' So he divided his property between them.

Not long after that, the younger son got together all he had, set off for a distant country and there squandered his wealth in wild living. After he had spent everything, there was a severe famine in that whole country, and he began to be in need. So he went and hired himself out to a citizen of that country, who sent him to his fields to feed pigs. He longed to fill his stomach with the pods that the pigs were eating, but no one gave him anything.

When he came to his senses, he said, 'How many of my father's hired servants have food to spare, and here I am starving to death! I will set out and go back to my father and say to him: Father, I have sinned against heaven and against you. I am no longer worthy to be called your son; make me like one of your hired servants.' So he got up and went to his father.

But while he was still a long way off, his father saw him and was filled with compassion for him; he ran to his son, threw his arms around him and kissed him.

The son said to him, 'Father, I have sinned against heaven and against you. I am no longer worthy to be called your son.'

But the father said to his servants, 'Quick! Bring the best robe and put it on him. Put a ring on his finger and sandals on his feet. Bring the fattened calf and kill it. Let's have a feast and celebrate. For this son of mine was dead and is alive again; he was lost and is found.' So they began to celebrate.

Meanwhile, the older son was in the field. When he came near the house, he heard music and dancing. So he called one of the servants and asked him what was going on. 'Your brother has come,' he replied, 'and your father has killed the fattened calf because he has him back safe and sound.'

The older brother became angry and refused to go in. So his father went out and pleaded with him. But he answered his father, 'Look! All these years I've been slaving for you and never disobeyed your orders. Yet you never gave me even a young goat so I could celebrate with my friends. But when this son of yours who has squandered your property with prostitutes comes home, you kill the fattened calf for him!'

'My son,' the father said, 'you are always with me, and everything I have is yours. But we had to celebrate and be glad, because this brother of yours was dead and is alive again; he was lost and is found.'" (Luke 15:11–32, New International Version [NIV])

The Parable of The Prodigal Son from the book of Luke in the Bible speaks clearly to me on many levels. I can identify with the son who wanted to strike out on his own. I wanted to, as well, when I was young, and although I did not lead a life of unconstrained debauchery, a life of pure innocence couldn't be claimed either. So identifying with the son in the story didn't present a large leap to me. And as I spoke of earlier, returning home at an older age to regroup made this an identifiable aspect.

My older brother stayed in our hometown, has always played by the rules, and lives a very stable life. Seeing his side of things as it relates to the parable isn't difficult either. Having younger sisters gives me the prospective of being the older brother too.

None of this really made that big of an impact on me until facing similar dilemmas this story told. My role as a father took on layers so much deeper than I ever considered. As a brother or son, the world seemed to revolve around me. When we are young, isn't that what most of us do? As I matured and became a bit more self-assured, it became easier to empathize with others and seeing life not only from my vantage point. Marriage and fatherhood drove that point home. My center now had to include them. Life was not exclusively about me (as if it ever had been). And as much as I would like to be completely self-centered, self-absorbed, and self-centric, that had to give way to the kids' self -centered, self-absorbed, and self-centric needs.

To many, this is a familiar teaching from the Bible. Countless books, sermons, talks, and discourses have been presented on it. Although I could not give an accurate percentage, my guess is that much of the attention is given to the young son who goes off, lives wildly, and returns a broken, humbled, and wiser young man. It is easy to see why. Notice the emphasis I have given to my one son's plight and entanglement. Why is that? Possibly, his story is juicier and makes it easier for us to look down upon him as we hold our own sanctimonious posture. We are given just enough information about the prodigal son to stimulate our imaginations, enough to know that he had crossed many lines of decent behavior leaving us with plenty of room to condemn him as his own brother had.

Mulling over this story, I kept thinking of the father and older brother. What were the discussions in the house during the young son's absence? Were there any? Did the mother or father ignore any feelings, or did they suffer silently until that fateful day of his return? Did the older brother display open hostility? Or did he just allow it to smolder and fester below the surface, not wanting to upset his parents any further by carrying on with being the dutiful son?

In the culture of the times, disowning a child and never speaking of him again happened to be quite common. The pain and sadness would have been suppressed, ignored, or endured. Would mother and father discuss and worry about him, or would they go on with little thought about him?

In our home the hope for a repentant son's return persisted. Any and all attention that we gave to Jeremy wasn't to the exclusion of the others. Sure, they were deeply hurt by all of this. There were measurable ramifications to their brother's problems. Their grades all went down when this all unraveled. A somberness and depression filled the house. We had just weathered a few tumultuous years, and now this seemed to be a punch in the gut. Life went on, and we adjusted to the new circumstances even with the undercurrent of the upheaval.

In many ways we are so fortunate. There are those who have lost forever, so much more. These are lessons that are individual to our own lives and are the fabric of our own individual life's tapestry. As I have discovered on this journey, nothing is secure and completely predictable. Comfort is fleeting. Nothing stays in the same position for too long. We adjust and move forward learning to forgive as we go.

Mother, father, and brother in the parable must have had mixed emotions going on. How could they not? Mother would cry for her baby boy. Father would maybe question his decision to acquiesce to his son's demand for his portion of the inheritance. To me, it isn't an inheritance until after the burial, but that might not have been their tradition. Father might have wondered if he had done the right thing. What led up to the demand? The son could have been so disagreeable and the father so fed up with his antics that getting rid of him would bring peace to the house. Seeing his son humbled and repentant might be the real reason he was so thankful of his boy's return. The boy had enough time to learn the value of things the hard way.

The older brother's reaction to the welcome home feast was to angrily stomp off in disgust and refuse to participate. Day in and day out he stayed home working and respecting his parents, knowing only that his brother was gone, leaving him to do both of their jobs. He saw the effect this had on his parents which only fostered his contempt for his younger brother.

But while big brother would not forgive, at least that we know of, father ran out not only to the returning son but later to shepherd his older boy back into the festivities. The father displayed to both of his boys the lessons of forgiveness, compassion, and mercy. Both might not be equally receptive to the lessons at the moment, nevertheless, the father did not withhold his love in any case. Nothing being withheld, the ring on the boy's finger allowed him to have family rights including money. Wrapped in the finest robe confirmed his position in the family would not be diminished.

The benefit of scrutinizing this particular parable allowed me to comprehend more than my emotions alone. The way each individual in my family felt would also be acknowledged.

The tricky part is not having this come off as a lecture. Any open and hope for discussion with my children sometimes curtailed as I watched their eyes glaze over with the invisible wall of "Yeah, yeah, yeah, I've heard this before" washing over them. I am still working on that.

A deeper understanding of my father and his choices concerning our lives gave me a greater appreciation of him because of this parable. It is a fine high-wire act we walk as parents. How do we guide and not offend or lead without demoralizing yet love unconditionally?

In the book *The Vortex* by Esther and Jerry Hicks, on pages 34 and 35, there is some guidance to the parents that states:

> *The more you see things in your child that you do not want to see—the more of that you will see. The behavior that you elicit from your child is more about you than it is about your child. This is actu-*

ally true of all of your relationships, but since you think about your child more than most others, your opinion about your child plays a greater role in his behavior.

If you could de-emphasize the unwanted behavior you see in your child by ignoring it—not replaying it over again in your mind, not speaking to others about it, and not worrying about it—you would not be a continuing contributor to the unwanted behavior.

When you hold anyone or anything as your object of attention, you are leaning in one of two directions: toward what is wanted—or toward what is not wanted. If you will practice leaning toward what is wanted when you think about your child, you will begin to see behavior patterns shifting to more of what you are wanting to see. Your child is a powerful creator who wants to feel good and be of value. If you do not take score in the moment and decree him otherwise, he will rise to the goodness of his natural Being.

When you are in a state of fear, worry, anger, or frustration—you will evoke unwanted behavior from your child.

When you are in a state of love, appreciation, eagerness, or fun—you will evoke wanted behavior from your child.

Your child was not born to please you.
You were not born to please your parents.

It is true that we are told that we need to talk about such things in today's society; but here it tells us not to speak and worry and even ignore the unwanted in favor of focusing on the wanted. By doing so, we take away the power of the negative thoughts and keep them from gathering momentum and festering.

Let's use games of any nature for an example. In any game it is important to get more, score more, and lift more; be longer, faster, and quicker; or be more accurate than the opposition. If we deemphasized and eliminated those things, there would not be any reward of victory. There would be no point in the games. The value of the reward holds an attraction that gives the sense of accomplishment, something that is wanted. Take away that enticement, and the power of the activity will soon dissipate because there is no allure in pursuit of no rewards, the something that is not wanted.

Very rarely are we motivated just to participate in anything that doesn't have a goal attached to the activity. Unwanted behavior receives a certain type of reward as does wanted behavior receive its due. Generally, poor behavior still evokes at least some type of reaction and is often perceived as preferable to no reaction. Remove the incentive, and shortly interest in continuing aimless activities will cease.

It is the same with people. If they are not producing a reaction, they will lose interest at some point and stop, because there is no payoff for their effort.

Many contend that the opposite of love is hate and the opposite of hate is love. The real opposite of those two is indifference. How long do you think I would have continued performing if, throughout my show and at the end of each performance, instead of applause, people stood up and walked out without even acknowledging my existence? No one likes to be ignored. It takes the energy out of the endeavor.

The Truly Important

My career in theater taught me the importance of entrances and exits. Some are spectacularly splendid and some with lights up or lights to black. Curtains and doors close or open. Appearances and departures from different directions happen with surprises, while others are expected, rarely any two with the same conditions attached. What occurs between those beginnings and endings is life.

How it gets filled and why we do what we do is still somewhat a mystery to me maybe because everything begins with a thought, not just one thought but many thoughts that manifest when action and emotion are added. I know the concept. It's still mysterious to me.

Beholding the first breaths of my children and the memories of those moments delight my senses to this day, each one providing a different perspective because of the uniqueness to them. Jamie was a C-section for frank breech and folded like a clothespin. Jeremy's birth, even though he presented in the typical and natural fashion, seemed a brand-new experience. Joshua came on the heels of a fetal demise, and the uncertainty that rested in the back of our minds caused the event to take on a much deeper meaning. Jenna too arrived with those same concerns as was with Joshua. One difference though is we knew the sexes of the previous children, and this time it remained unknown to us until birth. So to watch each take their first breath offered a distinctive vision of a miracle.

That miracle of birth was no less evident as when I held in the palm of my hand a perfectly formed premature baby girl with no life and no breath, with all perfectly formed toes and feet, fingers and hands, arms and legs and a little body, and head and face that were denied nourishment from an autoimmune condition in the womb. It's not once but two separate occasions and almost identical in age development. Even though our babies did not share our air, their journeys, though thwarted, reinforced my sense of awe in the process. What remains astonishing to me is that each little girl reflected our features and could easily be seen as ours. On those sorrowful days, we were so thankful that we had children to go home to. Tears and grief were softened by their presence and the gratitude of having them.

Seeing a baby's first breath is an astounding thing.

In my mime performances, I performed my version of a life cycle. Everything in it I had experienced except the death part. That had to be imagined. Going to a number of viewings of relatives at the funeral home being the closest I had witnessed death.

That all changed when my father passed away. He died at the age of ninety-one, so it could not be said to be an unexpected event.

Right up to the end, his mind remained sharp. My brothers, sisters, and mother gathered for the final week after he returned from the hospital. He faced the culmination of his life with no regrets, and if there were any, he spent no time considering them now.

Dad rarely went without shaving. A couple of days after his return from the hospital, I decided to give him a shave. Propped up and lathered up and with his eyes closed, I began shaving his neck with strokes of illogical design.

He held his hand up and gently admonished me, "One direction! Go in one direction."

This I did as I said back to him, "Oh, just like I do!"

As I concentrated on the better technique, he closed his eyes again.

"I hope I'm doing this right, Dad," I said trying to reassure him.

His eyes popped open, his head and hands lifted a few inches, and he said with a fearful intonation, "Is there any blood?" (He always hated the sight of his own blood.)

Startled, I said, "No!"

"Then you're doing it right," he said calmly as he relaxed his head and hands back down and closed his eyes again. I detected a little "gotcha" attitude with a very subtle, almost imperceptible smirk from him.

The shave and that little repartee stands as the exclamation point in my relationship with my dad, more than a few very special moments to tuck away like the handkerchief in a suit's top front pocket. While I had been shaving him, he drew me close and asked, "Did the picture come?"

I didn't know what he meant and asked him, "What picture?"

He shushed me as if he were telling me a secret. I told him I would find out.

I found out that the picture in their Florida home which had hung above the living room couch that mom wanted couldn't be carried in the car when they returned north after the house was sold, leaving Mom quite disappointed. But Dad and my brother-in-law John arranged to have it shipped up to New Jersey, unbeknownst to my mother, as a birthday present from Dad. The picture never arrived and now was at least a week overdue. John set out to track it down taking almost a day to untangle the problem but found that the picture sat in Newark Airport because of a wrong zip code. John finally retrieved it. In the morning of what turned out to be the last fully conscious day of my father's life, he presented the heretofore lost picture with everyone gathering around his bed, the belated birthday present to his wife of nearly sixty-six years. Tears streamed, hearts were filled, and emotions swirled. Reflecting on this gesture, it seemed that by the dotting of the "i's," he could now rest.

There were moments like that with each of us during that last week.

Each of us spent a few minutes with him later that day, saying our goodbyes. In the evening he told Mom he did not think he would make it through the night. He did but never awoke, sleeping through the day and then the following night. On that Sunday morning, we watched him take his last gentle, shallow breath. At home in his own bed lying below the etched glass cross that hung above it for years, he departed gently, quietly, and almost elegantly. A floral basket had been hung over the glass cross years before, hiding it from view until only a few days before the basket inexplicably fell onto the pillow next to Dad's head exposing the long disremembered cross as if beckoning him.

Only a few days earlier, when sitting at the foot of the bed with my sister Beverly, I saw sparkling lights dancing above him as he slept. I even looked away and then back again to see if I just imagined this. They were still flickering and in full daylight. From what I have heard, this is not that unusual. I asked Beverly if she could see these sparkling lights when Dad sat almost straight upright, something he had not been able to do at this point by himself. My guess is that the angels wondered why Dad tarried. And by tarrying, Dad seemed to tell the ethereal welcoming committee, "Not just yet." In retrospect, I believe he waited for the picture to arrive, representing a remarkable lifelong gift of love to my mother.

During the night following my seeing the flickering lights, I sat on the couch in the living room, around 1:30 a.m. Stillness filled the house as I wrote down these experiences of the vigil. Suddenly, I heard what sounded like someone coughed. It's nothing major, mind you, just a little cough of some kind. I put down my paper and pen and walked to the end of the hall to the opened door (it was left that way to monitor any distress signals). Mom and Dad's room on the right and the other half-opened door to the guest bedroom where two of my sisters were sleeping to the left were both dark. Peeking into Mom and Dad's room and seeing nothing amiss, I turned and looked into the guest bedroom. All were still. All slept. I turned back to look in again on Mom and Dad when a perceptible puff of air touched my neck and an audible voice next to my ear saying "It's happening" broke the silence. Thinking it one of my sisters, I looked around expecting to see one of them standing next to me.

At first I thought the voice might have been asking, "What's happening?" But once realizing to be completely alone in the hall, I felt convinced it wasn't a question but instead a matter-of-fact statement, "It's happening." Both of the two rooms remained still and dark as I returned to the couch in the living room to journal this new ghostly visitation.

To be born a gentleman is an accident.
To die one is an accomplishment.

We decided that Dad's memorial service would be held on their wedding anniversary about a month after he died. It would have been their sixty-sixth. It was my honor of delivering his eulogy followed by my playing one of Dad's favorite songs on the piano, "Stardust" by Hoagy Carmichael. Even now, playing this song will seem like a few minutes of me being with Dad, thinking he may actually hear me. One time, only a few months ago while wrestling with a particular problem (most likely about one of the kids), I decided to sit down and play "Stardust" and ask Dad for some advice.

"What would you do in this situation?" was the query to my ethereal father.

Astonishingly, he spoke to me. He absolutely spoke to me in a clear, audible voice, as though sitting next to me.

He quietly intoned, "Go ask your mother," at which point anyone within earshot of me might have heard a cross between a chortle and a guffaw as I spit out "Thanks a lot, Dad" and abruptly stopped playing to absorb the moment.

It was fun to tell my mother about what happened and why. Then I asked her if she could guess what he said.

Mom said, "He told you to ask your mother."

"How the heck did you know that?" I asked somewhat amazed that she knew exactly what he had said.

"Because," she answered with a laugh, "he never dealt with that stuff when he was here! That stuff has always been my job to help sort it out with you kids. He always said that. You didn't think he would change now, did you?"

Dad loved a shaggy-dog story. Some of his favorite storytellers were Bob Newhart, Andy Griffith, and a couple of radio comedians from the 1950s, 1960s, 1970s, and 1980s, named Bob Elliott and Ray Goulding, "Bob and Ray." Here is one of his favorite classic yarns Flip Wilson, the comedian, made famous which I have embellished in the retelling:

Ain't No News

The long journey back home took longer than usual this time. Business had delayed Mr. Barrett for nearly three weeks. Bad weather added another and the time to repair the broken wheel on his carriage yet another. His horses could sense the nearness of home. In unison they seemingly quickened their pace on the last long stretch of road before coming into view of the entrance that led to the remaining mile. Anticipation for the long overdue homecoming at main farmhouse grew as each familiar landmark came and went.

Mr. Barrett could see the neighbor's son, working on the dilapidated section of fence and slowed down by gently pulling on the reigns to bring the carriage to a halt next to the working boy.

"Oh, hello, Mr. Barrett, welcome home! We thought you'd be here sooner," the shirtless young man exclaimed as he stopped to wipe his brow.

"Well, William, I thought I'd be home sooner, too. These trips seem to get longer and longer. So how are things around here, any news?" Mr. Barrett enquired.

"Nope, ain't no news," William responded. "Excepting your dog died. Other than that there ain't no news," he added.

"Big Shep died? How did that happen?" Barrett questioned.

"Not precisely sure! Word is that Big Shep ate some bad horse meat, got sick and died!" was the reply.

"That's terrible! Just terrible! Where did Shep get bad horse meat?" asked the now not so weary traveler.

"Seems to me that the dead horse rotted in the sun after it died, your dog came along, ate the bad horse meat, got sick and died," stated William.

"What dead horse?"

"Yours!"

"Mine?"

"Yes sir, all your horses died in the fire. Couldn't get them all buried before the sun rotted the horse, and your dog came along, ate the bad horse meat, got sick and died," William answered.

"Fire, what fire?" blurted the astonished man.

"Why, the big one that took down your barn. The horses got trapped and couldn't get out. The fire burned the whole thing to the ground, it was a little too hot to clean up the horses so when the sun rotted them, the dog got to the bad horse meat, ate it, got sick and died," the young man said matter-of-factly as he sat down on the new fence rail.

"What? The barn burned to the ground? How'd the barn catch fire?"

The boy breathed one big sigh, shook his head side to side and said, "Everyone thinks the wind caused it."

"How the devil can the wind cause a fire?" asked an incredulous Mr. Barrett.

"Like I said, everyone else thinks the wind caused it. Me? I think the wind helped make the flames jump from the roof of the main house to the roof of the of the barn, causing it to burn down, killing the horses and then the sun rotted the horses because no one could get to them except your dog, but then he ate the bad horse meat got sick and died. Just like I told you earlier! But, no, I don't think the wind caused the fire. That came from the fire on roof of the main house." William finished with a shrug of his shoulders.

"The roof of the main house was on fire? Where did that come from?" the now dumbfounded traveler asked in an increasingly higher pitch.

"Flames shot up the curtains quicker than you could blink an eye, spread to the roof lickety-split, the wind kicked up throwing the sparks over to the barn, and being that the barn was so dry, it didn't take a whole lot of time for it to burn down, with the horses caught inside, making it impossible to get to them, because of the heat and all and when things cooled down a bit, it was too late for the dog who ate the sun bloated rotting horse meat, got sick and died."

Unable to restrain his infuriation, Barrett now demanded, "How, for Heaven's sake, did the curtains catch fire?"

"Well, it wasn't so much Heaven as it was the Preacher Johnson."

"Damn it William, why was Preacher Johnson at my house and what does he have to do with the curtains catching fire?"

"I was about to tell you, before you interrupted me. You see, the right good reverend accidentally knocked over the candle because the casket got moved too close to the window so that all the people could fit in the parlor. That's when the candle torched the curtains, and just like that, the flames climbed the walls because of the curtain and everyone went a running."

"MY God, boy, why was there a casket in the parlor? Who died?"

"You mean besides your dog and the horses?" William asked as he stood up from his perch.

"Yes! Yes! Yes! Besides the dog and the horses, who died?"

"Oh, that would be your wife. While you were away, she got sick something awful. The doctor came but couldn't do nothing and she died the next day. Word got around that you were out doing business and we all pitched in to give her a real nice funeral. Pa and me built the coffin, and it looked real nice with the table cloth on top, but I think that table cloth really sparked the curtains when Preacher Johnson bumped into the casket knocking the candle over when it was being moved next to the window to make room for everyone. Once that happened, the flames flew up those curtains and straight up through the ceiling, people running everywhere. In no time, the roof of the house lit up half this county, just then the wind started whipping and whipping, sending patches of fire over to the barn where the horses went crazy trying to break down those doors. But it was too late. That barn went up in a blaze faster than you can sing two verses of 'Amazing Grace.' Preacher Johnson was about to commence with that when all hell broke loose. People running everywhere and Preacher Johnson screaming 'I'm sorry, Oh Lord, forgive me, I'm sorry!' But everyone was screaming too, so I'm not sure if the Lord actually heard him. Anyway, the fire took days to cool down but not before the sun turned those dead horses rancid, and before anyone knew what happened Big Shep went and ate some of that bad horse meat, got sick and died. Too bad because I really liked that dog! Other than that, Mr. Barrett, there ain't no news."

To laugh often and much; to win respect of intelligent people and affection of children… to leave the world a better place… to know even one life has breathed easier because you have lived. This is to have succeeded.

—Ralph Waldo Emerson

CHAPTER

14

CHILDREN GROW AND
PARENTING NEVER STOPS

Throughout the course of writing this book of reflections and recollections, I noticed that many different conversations with a multitude of people, at some point in our interaction, somehow correlated to some aspect of this book. During the span of time covered in these pages, close to fifty years, many topics, thoughts, and ideas flowed and landed to tell an overall story. And like the conversations just mentioned, there may be more than a few that touches on something you may have encountered, experienced, or thought about.

An actor creates by using the events familiar to him or her by bringing them to the character in the best way they are capable. Parenting is much the same. In writing and performing my mime show, as with my acting, I attempted to bring common familiarities to life. The goal to evoke thoughts, emotions, laughter, tears, contemplations, compassion, and other viewpoints into the realm of consideration stood at the forefront of my intentions. Parenting, again, is much the same. We want others to understand who we are, why we think the way we do, and why we feel the way we do and to connect in some way to know we are not alone in our thinking. And at the very same time, we want to let it be known that we are of a different mix and stand out in a very unique way, holding onto those common threads that weave us together.

Passing on our histories, traditions, knowledge, thoughts, and dreams down to our children, or others maybe younger or maybe older than us, gives us a sense of meaning, a sense that our lives contribute to the bigger picture in the grand scheme of things.

Whether it is bringing a baby into the world witnessing its first breath or watching the last exhale of a long lived life, the experiences overflow with wonder and emotion. So it is with the mundane to the majestic, depending on the attention you assign to each happening.

Our impacts may appear small and minute at any given time, yet one seemingly insignificant utterance or gesture might bloom into a valuable influence in a person's life. Wouldn't it be nice if we could identify which ones and to whom they mattered? Of course, it is hoped that abundantly more positive examples reign, because the negative moments can have their say so too.

Martin Luther taught that it is not by works that we are judged, but faith. All of the accomplishments and accolades, setbacks, and missteps paint the nuanced portrait that is a life. I can only hope and have faith that I have designed something that is interesting, influential, and meaningful. With each stroke that I apply, as I get older, it is my desire to add to, not diminish from, the impression that is left.

So many of us believe that the work we do or the vocation we choose defines and embodies who we are. All are given gifts in this life. Part of our experiencing this life is to give those gifts a chance to blossom. I think this is only part of our life's meaning. Using our talents to express our viewpoint, visions, and dreams is an important aspect to our being. Yet, I believe it is how we learn to treat each other that will generate lasting impact as well. Who we are and who we become as individuals sometimes get overlooked in the equation.

How many times have we seen well-known people, though their works are deemed great, fall to the shame and humiliation of base thought and actions? No one is immune to making serious mistakes in life. It happens in lapses of personal judgment, in the blink of an eye, or in a series of miscalculated actions. Scandalous events can mark a person for life. Sometimes it can work for his or her benefit, but mostly will be the ruin of them in many ways. Things like this can attach to a name forever. It is a sad occurrence when this happens, but more importantly it is not how it affects their career, but how a person grows as a result. Wounds can heal, but scars never completely disappear. Long after the pain and suffering is gone, those scars can be used to remind us that such wrongdoing need not be repeated. There are no guarantees that even thoughtful actions won't offend someone at some time. Actions can be misinterpreted, certainly.

This is all part of the teaching parents do in preparing their children for the adult world. It is why youthful indiscretions carry less castigation. The quote "You can lead a horse to water, but you cannot make him drink" can be understood quite well in the raising of children. Teaching is one thing; learning is another. We all can relate to doing things that were not wise, sometimes foolish and many downright stupid. Some mistakes we came upon quite innocently. We rebelled against some warnings to our detriment. As adults, we pretty well know the ramifications, which is why we try to impart rules and boundaries for our children's guidance.

If they are not appreciated now, it is the hope they will be later. And in the case of the inevitable setback, hopefully we find the grace to forgive as we wish to be forgiven, because we sometimes bumble our way through situations, even while trying to do it right.

Parenting continues as long as we have children. Our effects can reach down generations. Although my father is now gone, his influence is still felt just as strongly as my mother's influence on this side of the great divide. Words and traditions from their parents still resonate and are being taught to my children. I am certain that many philosophies, ideas, wisdoms, and principles will reach on down to my children's grandchildren as well. And the same applies to you and yours.

Reflecting back to the earlier times in my life as a developing artist, through the ensuing years to convey my journey and its transitions, I did not know what it would reveal on paper. Just as a journey through life is filled with unknown destinations, so too is this parade of memories. Starting in one area of thought soon crossed over to other cogitations and musings. I knew I wanted to cover a period of time, but quickly realized the scope encompassed a variety of endpoints. As I mentioned in the earlier part of the book, a marksman benefits greatly by an actual target. My target aimed at providing insights that might prove interesting and maybe helpful to those beyond my current sphere of influence. My performances, for all intents and purposes, are gone, never to be duplicated exactly again. They lived in the world of "in the moment" experiences. Writing about them, I intended, would be a way of giving a little more permanence to that part of my life. My children represent, to a better degree, my existence, if not my importance. At least they are a solid manifestation of creations I took part in.

And so, in an attempt to leave a more enduring and indelible mark on the world, as well as a wish to reach into the future, I chose to write this document of sorts. Where its ultimate destination in the grand scheme of things happens to be is not up to me. I can only say that I did not back down from the personal challenge of putting down in words some of my adventures, foibles, shortcomings, tragedies, missteps, triumphs, and victories.

Since being an Olympic champion should, most likely, be off my "to do" list, I would gladly find contentment in adding to my resume "Best Selling Author." But again, I can only do my part.

How many of us have worked diligently, tirelessly for a dream, vision, or goal and did not achieve the satisfaction of seeing it to fruition because the reward suddenly seemed too far off to give the added energy that might have made the difference between success and incompletion? Did we quit on the cusp of triumph? I know there are times that will test my resolve to finish a project. The creeping in of self-doubt can be a paralyzing concept when given enough energy. Never mind the cacophony of noise created by the naysayers of the world singing in disharmony to celebrate failure since they will never attempt to savor the taste of success. Why? What holds people back? Fear of failure, fear of rejection, fear of success, or whatever reason that can be used is my understanding. Where focus of energy is, the result of that energy will help form the conclusion, good or bad.

Of course, other factors and ingredients contribute to any outcome. Look around your own life to see where added effort will produce your wanted results. How important do you rank those wants in your life? To that degree you will achieve them. Some ideas, like this book for me, start long before any action is applied. It is only when prioritized did something of utmost importance and highly valued in my life force this want to its intended level.

But before the prioritizing comes the dream. From the front of this book to the last, I speak of the dreams, visions, ideas, and thoughts that initiate the paths we choose of all lengths and widths. Where do we put more credence? On those embarked upon or those completed? Hidden in every venture are perils and pearls. How wonderful to be able to glide through the perils unscathed and enjoy the luminance of the deep rich pearl. Life isn't like that. What we sometimes forget is that the deep rich pearl started out a grain of sand and, by irritation, grew into a thing of perceived beauty and value and then needed to be discovered. And the perils test our commitment to the process, with some being of minor consequence, while others needing soul-searching dedication.

Finding joy from the inception through the journey itself and finally the satisfaction of its conclusion, and sometimes paying a heavy price to that end, we can only hope for the results we envisioned when we started.

I have tried to reveal the narrative of my unpredictable life, through its weavings, its offshoots, its setbacks, and also its victories, with love and humor touching on many proud moments and many painful ones. So many other stories will remain off the page for now or maybe forever.

As an actor, the little voice in the back of my mind that continually asked, "Do you really think your best is good enough?" had to be quelled with severe diligence. No matter what we do, we have that fearful thought that must be tamed and overcome. Every time I took the stage, even with confidence and evidence to the contrary, that voice had to be put in place. That little negative, nagging phantom in my head would not be the cause of my lack of trying. I do know that this is not the voice of God. Still, it does not stop the evil one who tries to influence through doubt in a bid to separate me from truth.

As a parent, the same voice attempts to undermine accumulated wisdom and teachings, again making it necessary to stifle that awful and destructive phantom.

So it is with writing this deeply personal chronicle. The further I have proceeded into this process, the louder that little voice has grown. I know it is not one to be listened to. And neither should you be deterred from what your heart says is right and true in your life.

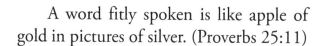

A word fitly spoken is like apple of gold in pictures of silver. (Proverbs 25:11)

I left my heart out on the stage for every performance, always attempting to get it exactly perfect knowing I might reach excellence in so doing. I have given my heart to my family and done the best I know how. The passage of time will determine my true merit.

Most of my performances of my solo mime show, *Body, Mime, and Soul,* concluded with me appearing on the stage carrying with me a towel, a mirror, and a makeup removal. I would smear the cream over my face and, looking into a shaving mirror, wipe away my mask while the audience watched the revelation of my true persona. With the exception of a blurted word during the performance, for effect, they had not heard me, only seen me. I devised this culmination for two purposes. The first is that I did not enjoy talking with people who came back stage after the show while I still wore my whiteface mask. And the second is that it allowed me to speak to the audience without doing so through the traditional silent symbol of that mask.

Before taking my bow, I felt it important to share a sentiment that reflects the privilege I believe it is to be able to do what I do for those people kind enough to spend their time in coming to see me perform. William Shakespeare wrote one particular sonnet that speaks to me and expresses exactly how I feel about the opportunity to perform. It seemed to be the perfect finale to my show. As with the show, I am grateful that you have spent your time on this part of my journey, thus making it a small part of yours.

Imagine now the lights fading to black on an almost empty stage, leaving me standing in a lone spotlight having just wiped away my mask, saying goodbye, and expressing my thank you to those I have touched. But now especially to my wife, my children, my brothers and sisters, and family and friends, I penetrate the silence with these words:

Sonnet 91
William Shakespeare

Some glory in their birth, some in their skill,
Some in their wealth, some in their bodies' force,
Some in their garments though new-fangled ill;
Some in their hawks and hounds, some in their horse;
And every humour hath his adjunct pleasure,
Wherein it finds a joy above the rest:
But these particulars are not my measure,
All these I better in one general best.
Thy love is better than high birth to me,
Richer than wealth, prouder than garments' cost,
Of more delight than hawks and horses be;
And having thee, of all men's pride I boast:
Wretched in this alone, that thou mayst take
All this away, and me most wretched make.

ABOUT THE AUTHOR

Millions have seen Ken Alcorn perform as a mime, an actor, a singer, and a musician over the years. He attended the American Academy of Dramatic Arts in New York and is a graduate of the University of North Carolina School of the Arts with a BFA in drama. He studied mime with James Donlon, Claude Kipnis, and Marcel Marceau.

Ken started out as a cocktail pianist in restaurants, has performed in over seventy-five plays and musicals, commercials, cabarets, and revues. He has taught mime and acting, directed, been an adjudicator in Virginia and Georgia for high school One-Act Play competitions, served on advisory boards, served as a deacon and has been a business owner, and has held the least appreciated job in the world for nearly three decades as a full-time parent.

Ken and his wife, Beth, are the parents of four young adults—James, Jeremy, Joshua, and Jenna.

For further information or to contact Ken Alcorn go to his website: *Bodymimeandsoul.com* or email: *Kwalcorn1@Gmail.com*

CPSIA information can be obtained
at www.ICGtesting.com
Printed in the USA
FFHW021036310119
50355109-55455FF